How To Play Golf

SAM SNEAD'S

How To Play Golf

AND PROFESSIONAL TIPS ON
IMPROVING YOUR SCORE

ALSO

Rules of the Game of Golf

AS APPROVED BY

THE UNITED STATES GOLF ASSOCIATION

AND BY THE

ROYAL AND ANCIENT GOLF CLUB
OF ST. ANDREWS

GARDEN CITY PUBLISHING CO., INC.
Garden City, New York

One of golf's most popular figures, "Slamming" Sam Snead, has just completed a decade under the big top. According to golf's foremost authorities, he is one of the finest "natural" golfers who have appeared in generations. It was under a Hot Springs, Va., dateline, September 20, 1935, that the following appeared in the newspapers of the country:

"Sam Snead, young local assistant pro making his debut in major competition, rocked par with a 68 this morning, then skidded downhill for a dozen holes, only to rally along the second-round stretch for a 76 and 144 total that brought him a three-shot lead in the $2,500 Cascades seventy-two hole open golf championship."

That paragraph blazed the trail of one of golf's most brilliant and entertaining luminaries. Snead's rise to fame was meteoric indeed. By 1938 he was top money winner

5

and was proclaimed the year's outstanding golfer and presented with the award emblematic of that distinction in the Court of Sport at the New York World's Fair. The presentation was made by George Jacobus, then president of the Professional Golfers' Association of America. The "honor guard" comprised such outstanding pros as Horton Smith, Byron Nelson, Ed Dudley, Leo Diegel and Dick Metz.

Snead dropped to sixth in the winter tour of 1939-40. He had embarked upon that tour under a psychological handicap for it was in June of 1939 that he had taken that disastrous 8 on the last hole of the seventy-two which had lost him the national open championship. The following year Snead had another disappointment when he was defeated by Byron Nelson in the final of the national P.G.A. at Hershey by the margin of one hole. Coming back to win that honor in 1942, his first national success, Snead found himself within a few days of entering the United States Navy. For two years Sam was out of competition but his come back was sensational.

Beginning the comeback at Portland where he was first with a score of 289 in the late winter of 1944 Snead tied for third at San Francisco, tied for seventh at Oakland, was first at Richmond with 278 and ushered in the season of 1945 by leading the field at Los Angeles. Later he won at Gulfport after a double tie with Nelson.

On top of this Snead captured the tournaments at Pensacola and Jacksonville, the latter marking his third straight medal-play victory. At Jacksonville he scored 266, which was 22 under par. Snead was in the semi-finals of the Miami four-ball matches and in the next medal play event, that at Charlotte, again tied with Nelson but this time lost on a double play off.

From Portland to Atlanta, in eighteen tournaments, Snead won $16,861. A broken wrist cost him dearly during most of the summer tournaments but he had caught up with the pack again by the time he reached Dallas in September, winning there by four strokes from a field that included Nelson, Hogan and McSpaden.

Samuel Jackson Snead's whiplash swing stands in the forefront of all for gallery appeal. In its flowing smoothness its power may be deceiving. Nevertheless it is the kind of swing the ordinary golfer seems to understand and most desires to cultivate. By staying in the top class he has demonstrated that his game is basically sound.

Fore!

THE FOLLOWING LESSONS are written in simple language so that the player can easily understand them, apply them to his individual swing, and quickly correct minor faults that may have developed.

They will aid the beginner in getting a clear idea of how the swing should be made, and will state reasons why certain fundamentals are adhered to, and what can be expected if they are not.

They are not written with the intention of making a champion out of all who read them, or with the idea that the golfer need not seek further instruction.

The answers to nearly all questions concerning the swing will be found in the following articles. By following their instructions, the player will more quickly grasp the ideas a professional instructor tries to convey, thus hastening progress in developing his game.

Contents

The Value of Instruction

IT IS TRUE that a player can bring his score down to what is considered good golf without instruction, but he never will be able fully to enjoy the game until he has developed a certain amount of consistency. The beginner should never go near a golf course until he has some idea as to how the ball should be hit.

The player who attempts to learn the game without instruction forms incorrect habits which are a handicap to satisfactory headway. This type of golfer prides himself on the fact that he is self-taught, little realizing that he is falling into errors that will be hard to correct when, and if, he has to see a competent instructor.

Such a golfer will improve to a certain degree, there is no doubt, but never will he be of championship caliber, and soon he will reach a stage where improvement ceases. Without a thorough knowledge of the fundamentals, he cannot achieve a high degree of efficiency.

It is an inconsiderable percentage of golfers who ever succeed in getting down to a point where they are scratch players.

Without a good instructor, golf looks easy to the beginner, and he thinks he can learn the game unaided. He fails to realize that to err is human, and that it is natural to do incorrectly the movements that are required to swing the club successfully.

To teach people how to play the game of golf as well as possible is my job — and that of all professionals — but since there are golfers who do not have the time or the means to obtain individual instruction I will try to present, in as few words as possible, the fundamentals of golf, and will try to impress upon the golfer the simplest reasons why this or that should be done to acquire a stroke that will give the player a certain degree of satisfaction, and start him on the correct path.

Your teacher, including myself, will get as much satisfaction out of knowing that we have helped you break a hundred or have brought your score down to an all-time low, as if we were doing it ourselves for the first time. Instruction is expendable if the player desires to get his game down to a point where he can give par or the best player in the club a good tussle.

Remember, when visiting your pro, each individual has certain peculiarities. His form is as personal as his handwriting. It is his alone.

Since all golfers are not built alike, they do not swing alike, and it is impossible to use the same standard methods to teach the short player that would be used to perfect a good swing in the taller player. The teacher can make alterations in the swing, to fit the individual style, without wandering from the basic fundamentals.

The pupil is the one who has the necessary mental and physical parts for the golf stroke, but it is only the good instructor who can assemble them so that they fit properly, are in relation to each other, are timed, and are in perfect harmony.

If there is any departure from the correct method of bringing the clubhead into the ball at the right angle, the golf instructor is capable of analyzing the cause and effect. Having made instruction of the Royal and Ancient game a profession and his business, the pro is well equipped with a sound knowledge and understanding of his subject. He is an expert in his field. You will soon note through association with your instructor that he is able to catalogue various causes for misplayed shots. For example, there is more than one reason why a shot is sliced. Each is caused by a variation from the correct method, be it a failure to keep the left arm straight, or an overpowering of the left side by the right. The pro readily can see and detect which fault is causing the clubhead to meet the ball inaccurately. After he has made the correction, the player then can practice, and be sure that he is not molding a bad habit by a continuous execution of the fault, hoping that the old feeling of good stroking will soon return of its own accord.

Tutorage under a competent instructor is worth much more than the slight remuneration you will pay him. You not only will be shown the correct method of swinging, but your stroke will be under constant scrutiny. This will keep your stroke in a constant groove, and your instructor will be able quickly to check a wrong before it becomes a habit.

It is my recommendation that the person who has never played golf first acquire, through a professional or through study and practice, a fair knowledge of the fundamentals of the swing. The game of golf is not just a case of hitting the ball around a pasture. It is scientific and it is based on proven facts and fundamentals. Teaching the beginner is easier for the professional than teaching a golfer who has played some. The novice has not as yet formed opinions of his own, nor has he started to construct an incorrect swing that must be torn down and rebuilt. The beginner heeds the advice of the pro, puts it to good use, and develops rapidly. It is hard to correct the player who has a slight knowledge of what the stroke is composed. This player has his own ideas and explanations for what he thinks is causing the trouble. It is hard to convince him that he is at fault. This player, perhaps, has taken lessons from more than one professional without giving any instructor a fair chance to do him any good. A golf lesson can only help if the player will practice what he is told and shown until it becomes a natural thing for him to do without requiring a great deal of thought.

See your professional at your earliest convenience so that you do not fall into the category of the player who is hardest of all to teach. He is the one that is always experimenting with his game, changing his grip and swing. Once established and approved by your instructor, you should never change your grip or any part of it that would alter your natural swing. A good knowledge of the fundamentals requires no changes that will throw your whole game out of alignment.

Your pro will teach you the fundamentals, get them firmly set in your mind, and, with intelligent practice, the swing will soon become automatic. It is then grooved.

The professional, aside from being your teacher, has your interests at heart. He wants to see you enjoy the game, play it to the best of your ability, and furnish you with the proper equipment to accomplish the best results. He is invaluable in aiding you in the selection of the proper playing equipment, and will keep you posted on the latest design and developments of clubs, balls, and wearing apparel. He will listen to your lamentations — why the putt didn't drop on the eighteenth, or why you hooked in the rough on the eleventh. He will be your father confessor of golf. Take your golf troubles to him.

Selection of Golf Equipment

A WORKMAN IS NO BETTER THAN HIS TOOLS, and it is a poor golfer who blames his, providing he has good equipment. Of course, if his clubs are outmoded, he then has fair grounds to blame his tools.

Proof that improvement in golfing equipment has improved the game itself, is to be had in the records of the National Open. Fred Herd, in 1898, won this classic with a score of 328. Ralph Guldahl, in 1937 at Oakland Hills, Birmingham, Michigan, registered 281, paring 47 strokes from Herd's mark. This was made possible only through improvement in equipment.

It has been a far step from the old gutta percha to the modern liquid center and tightly-wound ball. Modern methods have brought all manufacture to such a high standard that what was considered the tops ten years ago, is now outdated and obsolete. So it is in golf.

In the days of the individual club-maker, the design and the workmanship that went into a club was good. These gentlemen were artists at their trade. But where they could turn out one masterpiece, it was difficult, if not humanly impossible, to duplicate the stick once it was broken or discarded for other reasons. They could not fit a brassie or a spoon to a driver, so that each of the clubs would be in relation to one another, and would have the same feel.

Before the event of matched clubs, it was necessary to be a curio collector. The player selected one club from here and another from there until he had a set that was in close harmony. He sometimes spent a lifetime doing this, and still never achieved his goal.

Today, clubs are made to precision. Manufacturers make thousands of them that look alike, feel alike, have the same whippiness in the shafts, and are counter parts in other details — much in the same manner as the automobile manufacturer turns out automobiles of the same design. Matched sets are harmonized so that the feel of the No. 9 iron is the same as the No. 2 iron in relation to weight, length, and balance. Differently weighted or unbalanced clubs require different timing, but if they are of the same family, the swing for each is much the same.

If you are in the market for a set of clubs, it is best to consult your professional or a reliable store. Clubs must be fitted to the individual, much in the same manner as is a suit of clothes. The professional can advise you as to the proper length of shaft, and also the proper lie of the clubhead. If the shaft is not of the right length, the lie will be wrong. If the club is too short, the golfer then has to bend over too far in reaching the ball, and takes a position at address that is unnatural and uncomfortable. If the club is too long, the swinging arc is flattened, and greater accuracy is necessary to have the clubhead meet the ball at the correct angle. To be sure that you are properly fitted, the professional will have you take a natural stance and then note whether the clubhead lies flat or whether it is resting on its toe or heel. Many bad shots are caused by clubs turning in the player's hands as the toe or heel hits the ground.

Remember, the professional is as anxious as the golfer to fit clubs properly, for it gives the player confidence, and progress in developing a good swing is more rapidly achieved. The professional knows that a light club can be swung faster than a heavy one, and that if the club is too light, the player will exert extra effort in attempting to assist the club in doing its work. Alterations can be made by adding weight to the clubhead, but if the club is too heavy, the golfer will feel that the clubhead is dragging and, to speed it up, start hitting too soon. The important thing is to see that the swinging weight of the club is balanced, and that the club is properly weighted for the individual swing.

These reasons should show a golfer the value of good equipment. But there are still other reasons. The modern driver should have enough loft and a deep face, not like those of a decade ago that were shallow, requiring the ball to be teed close to the ground. The player will gain confidence with this type of club as he can tee the ball higher, and this will give him the feeling that it is impossible for him to miss the ball. On the other hand, the brassie and the spoon will, and should, have a shallower face and more loft to be able to fit snugly against the ball lying on the fairway. The grips should be such that they fit the hands, tapering near the end so that the left hand will have the feeling of firmer gripping.

Depending on the player's swing, the shafts selected should be stiff or whippy. If one is a rapid swinger with considerable wrist action who hits the ball hard, stiff shafts are advisable. But if one is a slow swinger, more action will be put into the clubhead by a shaft that is flexible. The older player will benefit by having his clubs fitted with a whippy shaft. He will find the club doing more of the work, fatigue will be lessened, and the round will not require the physical stamina that it has in the past.

Proper attire is almost as important to good golf as proper equipment. Experience has taught the golfer that freedom of legs and arms, and a free turn of the torso are essential to proper swinging. One must be comfortable to execute correctly the movements of the golf swing. Shots call for concentration, so if the golfer is properly attired, he need not worry about this or that being out of place, which is bound to distract his mind from the shot. Designers have noted that clothes for golf should be loose fitting, and have added pleats here and there so that the player will be comfortable, and thus be enabled to get freedom in the swing.

In a book by Glenna Collett Vare, she tells of the woman who was playing a match wearing a knitted dress. In those days, women were wearing dresses quite a few inches longer than today. A terrific storm blew up, soaking this woman to the skin, and causing the dress to sag until it was trailing on the ground. Her morale was upset, and the self-assurance that the well-dressed woman has, was lost. This resulted in her losing the match despite having been several holes ahead.

Today a player can obtain weather-proof clothing, not only jackets, but trousers and wrap-around skirts as well. The golfers that play a lot should have these accessories strapped to their bag.

Shoes are an important item. They should fit well and by all means should have spikes. It is impossible correctly to execute the stroke when the feet are not well anchored and the player is continually thinking and worrying about his feet.

Importance of Proper Grip

Importance of Proper Grip

THE HANDS are the key station transmitting power from the body to the club. The grip is the connection in this central office that must be sound, for a faulty connection cannot transmit the impulses of the body, no matter how good they may be. Therefore, the grip is the all-important fundamental of the stroke. In it the final control of the club rests.

Proper gripping is essential if the clubhead is to meet the ball squarely. The hands must not be turned over to the left so far that the face of the clubhead strikes the ball while it is in an open position; neither should the hands be turned over too far to the right so that a rolling action of the hands at impact hoods the club. They should be placed in relation to the shaft so that in working together, providing the action of the body is correct, they will bring the clubhead into the ball at right angles to the desired line of flight.

We will assume that the proper grip is that which has been generally adopted by the better class of players. It was first molded by Harry Vardon, and bears his name. It is also called the overlapping grip. Vardon placed his left hand on the club so that a "V," formed by the index finger and the thumb of the left hand, pointed over the right shoulder. This brings the left hand in a position to offer a restraining resistance to the right hand that is constantly trying to overpower it. It also gives the golfer a firmer grip with the fingers than when the club is gripped by the palm of the hand.

The right hand is placed so that it will be free to exert extra effort when called on to whip the clubhead through the ball. It is not too far under the shaft so that a wrist snap is halted, but in a position in which, were the palm of the hand open, it would be presented to the hole, or in a plane at right angles to the intended line of flight. The "V" formed by the index finger and the thumb should also point over the right shoulder.

Since the hands should work in unison, they should be united either by an overlapping of the index finger of the left hand by the little finger of the right, or by interlocking the two fingers.

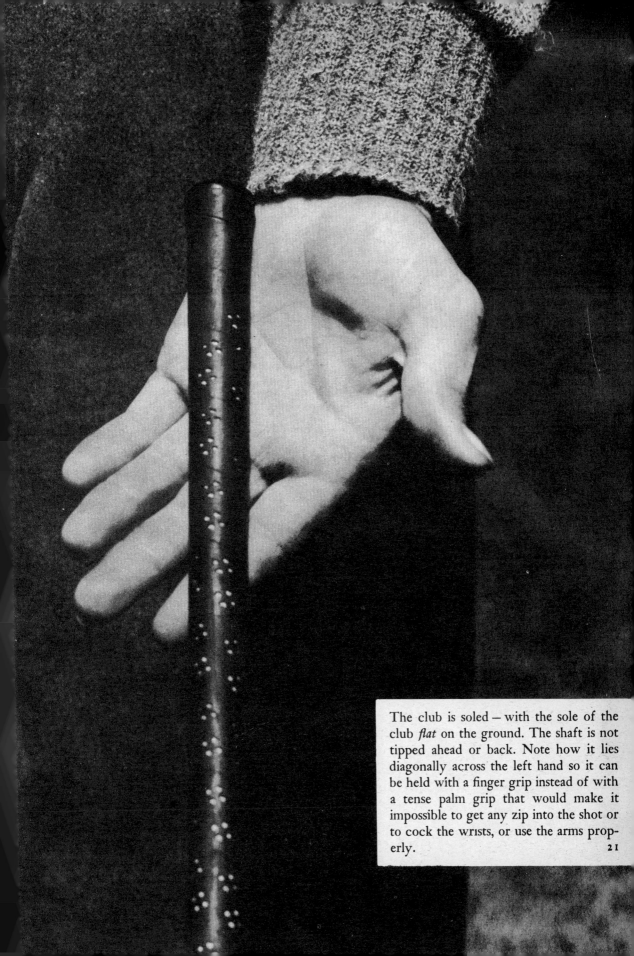

The club is soled — with the sole of the club *flat* on the ground. The shaft is not tipped ahead or back. Note how it lies diagonally across the left hand so it can be held with a finger grip instead of with a tense palm grip that would make it impossible to get any zip into the shot or to cock the wrists, or use the arms properly.

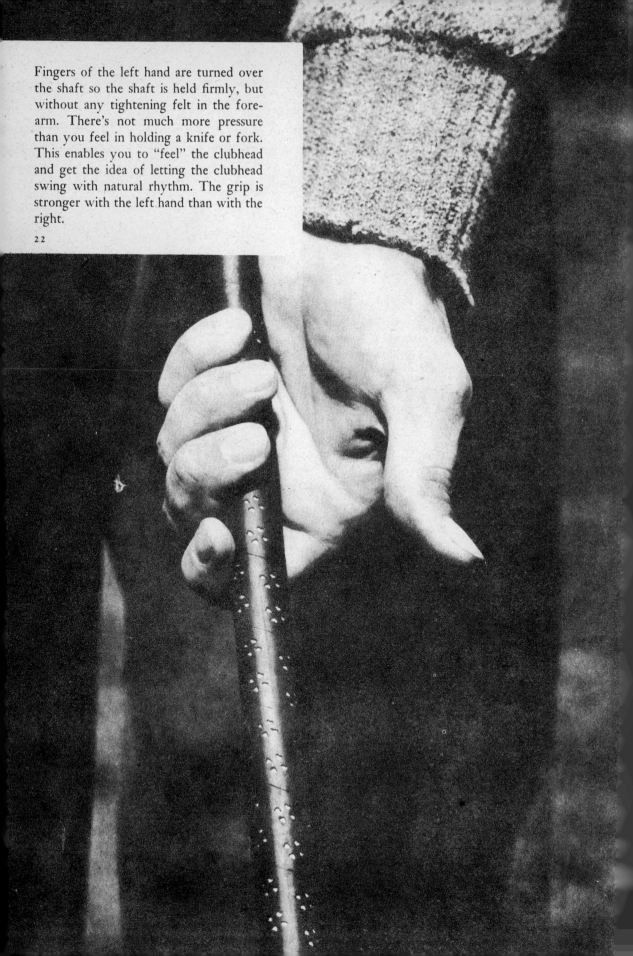

Fingers of the left hand are turned over the shaft so the shaft is held firmly, but without any tightening felt in the forearm. There's not much more pressure than you feel in holding a knife or fork. This enables you to "feel" the clubhead and get the idea of letting the clubhead swing with natural rhythm. The grip is stronger with the left hand than with the right.

22

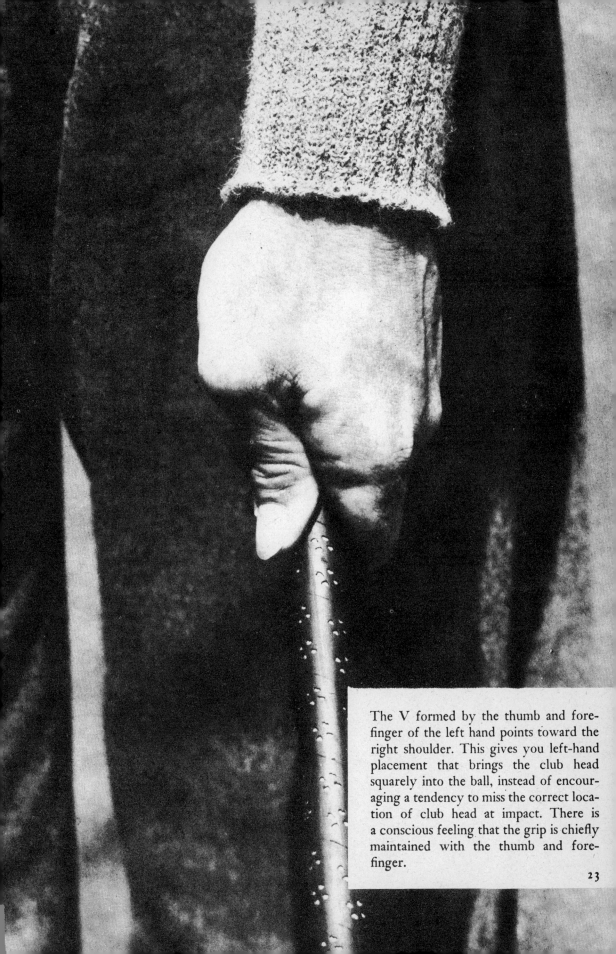

The V formed by the thumb and fore-finger of the left hand points toward the right shoulder. This gives you left-hand placement that brings the club head squarely into the ball, instead of encouraging a tendency to miss the correct location of club head at impact. There is a conscious feeling that the grip is chiefly maintained with the thumb and forefinger.

23

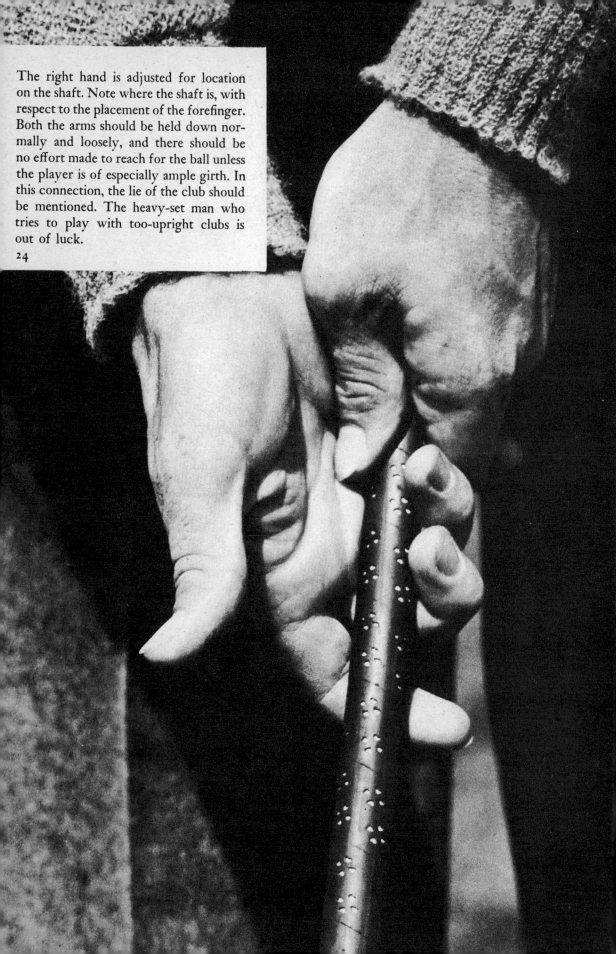

The right hand is adjusted for location on the shaft. Note where the shaft is, with respect to the placement of the forefinger. Both the arms should be held down normally and loosely, and there should be no effort made to reach for the ball unless the player is of especially ample girth. In this connection, the lie of the club should be mentioned. The heavy-set man who tries to play with too-upright clubs is out of luck.

24

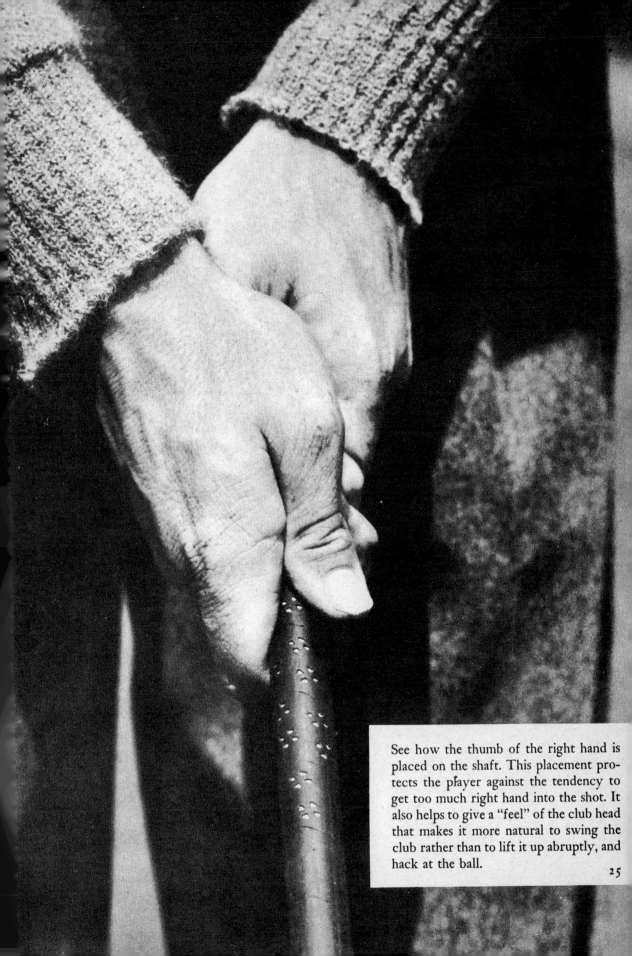

See how the thumb of the right hand is placed on the shaft. This placement protects the player against the tendency to get too much right hand into the shot. It also helps to give a "feel" of the club head that makes it more natural to swing the club rather than to lift it up abruptly, and hack at the ball.

25

Notice that the little finger of your right hand lies on top and across the first finger of your left hand. This grip I've been explaining may feel a little awkward for a while but practice with it, and you'll soon agree that it helps your shots.

26

Thrill of Good Wood Shots

THE TEE SHOT is probably the most important in golf, for a good start is half the battle. Being able to use the wood off the tee gives the player confidence, to say nothing of the satisfaction and thrill he gets in seeing the ball gradually climb from the tee and travel straight down the fairway until it seems that it is about to roll out of sight. A good shot off the tee will put the golfer in a proper mental attitude to play the second shot well. If his woods are off and he is always forced to make recovery shots, his interest in the game soon wanes and he becomes careless. Playing shots half-heartedly, he soon falls into bad habits. The shorter woods should also receive their share of attention. With them the golfer can often make up yardage that would be lost if he had to rely on an iron to hit the ball with any amount of success. The woods are the clubs to use when distance is required.

Various Uses of Wood Clubs

WHEN PLAYING A WOOD SHOT, remember a straight ball pays off over the one that is slugged farther but winds up in the rough. Instructors will always warn the novice against trying to hit too far. To achieve distance, the player should try to swing more freely; then the movements will be more accurately made. The more accuracy, the farther the ball will travel. Any form of pressing will cut down distance.

There is no question that the shot off the tee is more easily made than one made when the ball is lying on the fairway. The ball is more easily struck, and no unusual demands are made on the player when it is set up well. When this situation presents itself on the fairway, the stroke used off the tee is the one to use — striking the ball well in the back so that it will run. But when the ball has found a difficult lie, there are variations that must be made, and the sweeping shot used off the tee will not always get the ball into the air. The brassie shot off the fairway must be played from where it lies. This is one disadvantage over the tee shot, where the player can select the position and placement of the ball.

There are times when the golfer will find that his ball is not setting up well, and that he cannot rely on the stroke he used off the tee. If the lie is close, he should study it to see if a wood shot is justified. The chances of failing are great, if the lie is too close to use a wood; the player then would be better off to use an iron. For a wood, there should be a clear path for the clubhead to swing into the ball. If the lie is cupped, the iron should be used, for with its more upright swing, the clubhead can be brought down sharper and the ball can be more solidly hit than if a wood were used with a blow that has a longer arc.

The golfer confronted with a close lie should hit down with the brassie. To get a brassie shot up, the same rules apply as in getting an iron shot into the air. It is the loft of the club and a downward blow, plus backspin, that will cause the ball to rise. The ball will not rise as quickly as when hit with an iron, so be sure there is enough room in front. If there is not, the player should use the spoon or No. 4 wood. Needing a longer stroke than the iron, the brassie rarely takes a divot, but just strips the sod in front of the ball.

If there is any doubt as to whether the brassie should be used on a particular shot, it is better to use the spoon. The spoon, being a shorter club, will bring the golfer closer to the ball and the swing will be more upright. Naturally the ball will have to be played slightly more toward the right foot so that it can be caught while the clubhead is still descending. A good position for the ball is at a point between the center of the stance and the left heel.

It is important when playing shots off the fairway to start the backswing smoothly, and not to hurry the downswing. Free the body of any tension that may have crept into it by the thought that you are going to miss the shot; have the same confidence as you would off the tee, where the ball is teed up. It is true the latter is easier, and that swinging is much smoother and a more simple matter, but if you will remember the important thing about golf — to get the ball up in in the air, hit down on it — you will soon gain the necessary confidence, and shots off the fairway will cease to worry you.

The Stance

BALANCE is the very beginning of any golf shot. Stand with your weight evenly divided and your legs not too far apart. Turn the toes of both feet outward because this helps you retain good balance throughout your swing. Have your arms hanging freely so the movement of your body doesn't interfere with your arms. The ball and the hands are practically in the same vertical plane.

I drive with a slightly open stance; with the left foot a bit farther away than the right one from the line of intended flight. Others prefer a square stance, with both feet equi-distant from the line, and there are many excellent players who use a closed stance with the right foot farther away from the line. This, so the champions of the closed stance maintain, makes it easier to hit from inside the line of flight in an arc out into the ball. Such an arc, of course, is proper, except in the cases of deliberate slices and "cut" shots.

Note that the knees are loose in the address.

A few waggles to get loosened up, and to get the flow of the swing started without a jerk, are really an important part of the swing. They help you to feel the beginning of a smooth swing. Then you easily work into the first stage of the swing, which is illustrated here.

A slight lift of the left heel starts the hips rotating away from the shot. The left arm is held straight, practically as an extension of the shaft. There is no effort at all made to lift the club from the ground. The club head is kept low.

The left knee begins to bend slightly toward the right and there is a noticeable straightening of the right leg, although there should be no feeling of the right knee locking.

In this initial stage of the swing the prevention of tightening up is highly important. You can make many perfect swings clipping dandelions and scraps of paper, but when a golf ball is before you you're apt to become tense to a degree that completely destroys your precision. Take it easily and lazily, because the golf ball isn't going to run away from you while you're swinging.

Get your "master eye" drawing a bead on the ball. This determines the proper position of your head. Being careful about sighting your shot helps you, subconsciously, to concentrate. Your head will stay still enough if you do the other things right.

The Drive

The ball in this series of pictures on the drive appears to be played almost even with the right heel, although the angle at which the picture was taken accounts for that. The ball actually is played slightly ahead of the center of the stance.

See how the left shoulder and hip begin to slide downward and around as on a banked turn of a track. It greatly simplifies it for the average player if he will think almost altogether about left side performance in the earlier stages of instruction, because it is the left that seems to be the major factor in precision.

Note how balance has been maintained from the feet upward. The right foot is firmly planted and the inside of the left instep is pushing the hips around in their pivot. Note, also, how the left knee stays in the same horizontal plane instead of dipping as it does so frequently in the cases of high-handicap players.

Now the hands and arms begin to do some deliberate work in completing the backswing. Keep the left arm as straight as it is naturally, but don't tighten up by trying to get a feeling of tensity in that arm or you'll be inclined to take it out of the shot and do the rest of the work with your body, and get a dead swing.

The body continues to swing around, as may be observed by study of the position of the right leg in this picture and the one preceeding. The left arm is bent slightly but retains a feeling of downward tension. Note the position of the hands, virtually the same as in the address. No roll of the forearms has occurred.

Note how the wrists are beginning to cock. The wrists have no power; they are only hinges. However, when the club head is being swung in the proper path and with increasing momentum it's essential that the wrists work in a way that keeps the left arm straight and keeps the right elbow close to the body.

As the top of the swing is neared the player's hips have completed almost a 90 degree turn from the address position. This isn't possible for the older and less supple player, but the cocking of the wrists as shown, is not difficult, and it is important for securing power and firmness in the shot.

33

Note that the shaft of the club has begun to drop below horizontal. That also is something that isn't advisable for the less flexible player, although the fullest extent of a wrist-cocking that can be attained without losing control of the club, is highly desirable.

Here the major feature is from the hips up, with the shoulders coming around. There is a feeling of a definite pull on the left shoulder and arm. The knees are bent to allow freedom that promotes speed on the downswing. The angle of the wrists with the forearms is the same as it was at the top of the backswing.

You will note from the position of the knees that the downward motion of the body already has started, although from the position of the hands and club shaft it is plain that the club has just reached the farthest point of its backswing. A common error is to start back with the arms before the pivot has been completed.

Now the hips are almost parallel with the line of intended flight. The wrists have begun to straighten out into line with the arms. Note how the right elbow is down, and stays comfortably close to the body.

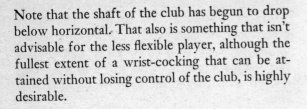

Now note how the knees are beginning to bend in a sort of a "sitting down to the ball" position, while there has been only a very slight change in the position of the club. The fraction of a second pause at the top of the backswing is caused unconsciously and is a sign that the wrists are not beginning to break too soon.

The left leg begins to straighten so it will be in the same position as at address. The wrists are snapping into a straight line with the arms so the club head will be brought through its wide arc, into the ball at the right time. This hand action has brought the shoulders around properly.

See how the left heel is settling down to a firm anchorage. From watching all the good ones hit, I've got the idea that this is one of the very important details of the long shotmaking. Simply getting that left foot well planted seems to be the action that controls the rest of the leg and body performance.

See how the right leg seems to be shoving power into the shot. The camera angle of this shot is misleading. Actually the ball, the hands, and the left shoulder are almost in a straight line, as they were at address. Note how the right shoulder has dropped and the left one raised, as the swing approaches a vertical plane.

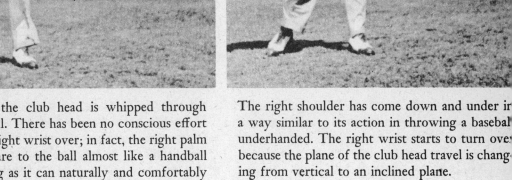

Note how the club head is whipped through after the ball. There has been no conscious effort to roll the right wrist over; in fact, the right palm is kept square to the ball almost like a handball shot, as long as it can naturally and comfortably stay square.

The right shoulder has come down and under in a way similar to its action in throwing a baseball underhanded. The right wrist starts to turn over because the plane of the club head travel is changing from vertical to an inclined plane.

It's simply a matter of smoothly "coasting" now. The hips start to turn square to the hole.

Observe how the hands finish high. In the case of a smaller and heavier player, the finish would be at a lower point.

See how the hips continue to be almost in the same position they occupied when the club head met the ball. This means that the body has stayed behind the shot, and is an indication that the club head has been lashed through the ball with the hands and arms.

The follow-through has reached its effective maximum in indicating that all possible power and control has been given to the shot. See how firm the left and right feet are staying to the ground, thus giving evidence that balance has been retained.

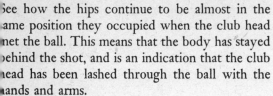

See how gradually the head has been brought up. There has been no jerking upward of the head by incorrect action of hands and arms.

The club finished far around because there has been no tendency to "brake" the club after the ball has been hit. Momentum carries the club.

The arms are hanging easily and almost straight down. The club is soled flat on the ground. There is no aspect of tensity about any phase of the starting position.

The Drive SIDE VIEW

Up to this point there has been no conscious movement of the hands. They have followed the pivot automatically. Note, especially the way the hips are swinging around in response to left leg impulse.

Note that the feet are in a line parallel with the line of intended flight. However, it suits some players to have either the right or left foot slightly farther away from the line, for drives and other shots.

Watch how the position of the hands is kept low. The club head is started back by the left leg beginning the pivot. The left shoulder and arm follow the action from the foot up.

Here's where the cocking of the wrists begins. See how the left foot shows that the swing is depending a lot on pressure from the ball of the left foot.

By comparing the position of the club head here, with that in the preceding picture, you get the idea of how far a slight cocking of the wrists moves the club head.

The right elbow is held close, but not tightly, to the body; with the elbow pointing down. Watch how the back of the left hand keeps approximately parallel with the face of the club.

See how the left shoulder and the left forearm position show the way to get a long sweep that is a necessary item in getting a powerful shot. Watch, too, how the right leg is braced as the axis of the swing.

Observe that a sort of a "sitting down" action has taken place. This prepares one for getting the body "punch" timed along with the legs, arms, and wrists, and protects against tensity.

Now the left leg has begun to straigten out so the hit can be made on a firm axis. The left shoulder is still under the chin but is drawing the club head down. Wrists continue to be cocked.

The wrists have done almost all of the moving of the club head that's been accomplished since the previous picture. They're getting into position for uncocking to whip the club head at the ball.

Note that the club head, wrists, and arms are about in the same position as in the previous picture, but that body action has started, as is evident from comparing knee positions. The downswing starts with the left leg.

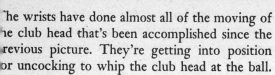

At this point both feet are flat on the ground to provide a good balance for the club head speed to increase without throwing the club head out of focus on its target. Here is where you want to begin uncocking your wrists.

Note how far the shoulders have moved since the preceding position, but with the wrists in the same relative position. Compare this picture with the one just ahead of it. The wrists uncocking have brought the club head through space too fast for the camera to catch the club head. Note how the left leg is braced. **41**

There has been a straightening of the right leg and a full lash in uncocking the wrists as the ball is hit. See how close to a straight line the left shoulder, hands, and club head are.

The ball is on its way and the club head point after it. You can see in this picture that plenty o power has been poured into the shot by the righ arm, but that it's kept in line by the straight lef

See how the head has been brought up naturally. What makes the head jerk up prematurely generally is faulty arm action rather than a hasty curiosity to see where the shot has gone.

The grip remains firm all through the swing, in cluding the follow-through.

42

Observe that the hips have been almost in the same position for the last four views. That means the hitting has been done from a hub that has stayed fixed in about the position of the base of the spine.

The right arm is staying just as straight as the left one did on the backswing. The wrists are turning over because they have to; the momentum of the club head swinging around and up makes them.

The second half of the follow-through comes automatically. If it's easy and approximately in the path of these pictures, it's a tip-off that the back-

swing and hit were correct. The follow-through is, in many respects, a reversed pattern of the backswing.

43

Action of the Feet

A PROFESSIONAL can look at a player's feet in action, and can nearly always tell what is wrong with the stroke. Foot action is one of the main differences between a good golfer and a duffer.

As the hands reach about halfway in the backswing, correct foot action has the weight of the body shifted against the right foot. The left heel has left the ground, with the ball of the left foot maintaining the balance.

At this same position the duffer makes the mistake of shifting all the weight onto the right foot by a lateral hip movement. When the top of the swing is reached, the left heel is drawn so high that the foot is almost at right angles to the ground. The toe then supports only the weight of the foot, rather than aiding the ball of the foot to grasp the ground and maintain balance. Starting the downswing with the feet in this position, the duffer can only make the fatal mistake, "failing to return the left heel to the ground." The left foot then is not in position to receive the weight about to be thrust upon it. When the weight is kept on the right foot the hips cannot turn out of the way to allow the hands to swing past. With the hips blocking the hands, power is lost.

When foot action has been faulty the duffer is hitting flatfooted. The expert on the other hand finds that at impact the right heel has left the ground and the foot is pushing against a resisting force. Although terrific force thrown against the left leg in the downswing may slightly roll the left foot over, it is firmly set, receiving the weight which has been shifted against it.

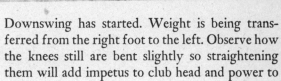

A perfect shot and follow-through will leave one in a well balanced position.

Foot and leg position at the top of the backswing. Note location of ball for wood shot. See how the pressure is being applied from the ball of the left foot. Left knee is swung to the right; not dipped.

Downswing has started. Weight is being transferred from the right foot to the left. Observe how the knees still are bent slightly so straightening them will add impetus to club head and power to the shot.

Set for the shot. The left leg is straight and the hands are whipping the club head through. Note how the hips are sliding through, rather than turning, as compared with previous position.

See how the hands are kept going after the ball with all power being applied in a "streamline," instead of stopping on the shot, as is a common fault. Note the right leg straightening to take left hip out of the way.

45

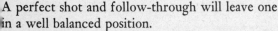

The Long Irons

ONE MIGHT CALL IRON PLAY the fine part of the game. A golfer does not slug with irons as he does with woods, nor does he try to achieve great distances. Iron clubs are designed for accuracy, and that should be the aim when playing them. The shafts are shorter than those fitted to the woods — necessitating a stance closer to the ball to provide for a rounder and more upright swing.

The No. 1, No. 2, and No. 3 irons are called the long irons. It is true that they are used to attain a certain distance, but the distance is considerably less than that which can be acquired with the woods. They are the clubs to use when the lie on the fairway does not permit the use of the wood club, and yet a maximum distance is desired.

Some golfers prefer to use a No. 4 wood in preference to the long irons. It is a good club to use on a calm day, for the degree of pitch of the club will send the ball high in the air, and a green can be held. But if the elements are disturbing, it is far safer to use the long iron. The ball is hit lower and the wind effect on the flight of the ball will be lessened.

Since the stroke is one in which the ball is struck a downward blow, there is a minimum chance that the ball will be sliced or hooked. If correctly hit, the backspin applied to the ball will hold it on the correct line.

When to Use the Long Irons

IRON PLAY is the core of the golf game. It is the middle stroke on which a continuation of the success off the tee depends, or on which a handicap from that spot is overcome. This shot requires more skill than the stroke played off the tee. It is a shot that requires considerable thinking. It demands mental calculation in advance, so that the player will have a definite object in mind.

The long iron is used when the shot calls for distance, plus accuracy, and it stresses the latter. It is the club that gets you there, if the right club is used for the right distance.

A straight-faced club is used when the lie is so close on the fairway that the use of a wood is prohibited. Being a shorter stick, greater accuracy is attained with it.

Irons are played for position, and if the shot is more easily played with a longer iron, that is the club to use. Avoid under-clubbing. A mashie-niblick, with a full swing, should not be used when the shot calls for a mashie with a three-quarter swing; neither should a No. 5 iron be used when the mid-iron is called for.

A half swing with a club suited for the distance is far more likely to be accurate than will be overswinging with a club not designed for the length. The shorter the swing, the more accurate will be the shot. There is little glory in hitting a 180 yard mashie shot. The idea is to see how close to the pin you can put the ball.

The long iron is a good club to use when the shot has to be played into the wind. The straight face will keep the ball low where the elements will not have the effect they have on a shot hit higher into the air. Clubs are designed with a variation of ten yards distance, so it is a good idea, when playing against the wind, to use a club one mark stronger than that used on a calm day.

In the long iron play, a loose grip must be avoided. You might get away with a looser grip off the tee, but here a firm grip is very necessary. Since the shock is greater in hitting the iron, a loose grip often can cause the club to turn in the player's hands.

The stance for iron play has an important part in achieving the desired results. An open stance is used because the goal is not distance. This stance shortens the backstroke and the pivot and the backswing become more compact, giving the player greater accuracy.

The long iron shot differs from the wood in that the stance is closer to the ball — a position necessitated by the shorter shaft. This brings the body closer to the ball so that the swing is more upright. Greater accuracy is then obtained. The ball should be played from a position in which it can be hit a downward blow. The upright swing makes it easier to do this than if the arc of the swing is a flat one.

Fundamentals of the swing are the same. The club should be taken back slowly and close to the ground, and the downstroke should be started in the same manner as with the wood.

Although the turn of the hips is restricted, do not consciously shorten the backswing; there should be a full and free shoulder turn. At the top of the swing, the position of the club is similar to that for the wood, but the hands should never go back beyond the shoulders. As already stated, this shot is not one for maximum length. That is achieved with the woods.

The long iron is one of the most important shots in the game, for if it is played well and onto the green, an extra chip shot is not necessary.

The stance is not quite as wide as for the wood club shots. The ball is about 3 inches back of a line to the left heel. Your grip is slightly stronger than with a wood shot, but not tense.

Keep the club head low when you're swinging back, and you'll be sure to swing, instead of trying to pick up the club and chop at the ball. See how the head is cocked and left eye is drawing a bead on the ball.

The Long Irons

Note how the left shoulder has come around under the chin. The head has been held still as you can see from inspecting that showing of shirt above the neck of my sweater. No reason for the head to move; the legs, body, and wrists are doing the work.

Here you see where the correct grip shows its importance. There is no rolling of the wrists so the club head is held in position.

50

Note the straight line from the left shoulder to the club head. Try to remember that and you'll overcome the temptation to lift the club with your hands. The picture angle shows the ball farther back than it really is.

The wrist cocking begins at this point (just as in the wood club swing). Study the way the legs work so the right hip swings easily out of the way, and permits a free, smooth swing.

See how the left arm is held out straight, so the fullest arc of the backswing can be secured. The whole idea of the backswing is to windup for a release of power without any jerkiness, going or coming.

Observe how the wrists have cocked almost 45 degrees from the preceding picture, while there has been relatively little change in the rest of the elements making up the backswing.

You can see from this picture that the action of the right hip shows a rotation instead of a swaying back along a fairly straight line away from the ball. This proper action makes it easier to hit harder.

You will see that the shaft of the iron club doesn't go much lower than horizontal and the pivot for the irons is less than for the woods.

See how the left arm is stretched to the full length of its leverage in providing power for the shot, and to avoid any change in the path of the club head that might result from an uncertain angle in the elbow.

See how the legs are beginning to straighten up from a "sitting down" position so the hit may be made with the left leg firm and straight. Notice, also that there has been no uncocking of the wrists. The ball is under the head. There is no swaying of the body.

Note that both wrists are under the shaft at the top of the swing. All these pictures are separated by the same time interval, so you will observe that there is a pause of the club head at the top of the swing so the downswing will be smooth.

Watch the knee action in this series of pictures. You will see that the body has begun its action for the downswing while the hands continue to be held at the top. Many players lose power and control by starting the hands first on the downswing.

At this point the swing path becomes more vertical. The body has about completed its work of swinging around on the hips and begins to set itself, so the hand action can proceed smoothly and whip down at the ball.

When the shaft gets at this point — level with the ground — then the wrists begin to shoot the works. From this stage of the swing down to the point of impact comes a good part of the power of the shot which results from speed of club head travel.

The club head is traveling too fast for the speed camera to catch because the wrists have lashed the club head at the farthest point of the swing's arc. Note how the right arm has straightened out to keep the club head in the right path.

See how the left hip is rising, rather than rotating. That means the left leg has been kept straight as a fixed point for the critical center of this part of the swing. The wrists haven't rolled. The back of the left hand is square to the line of flight.

Observe how balance has been maintained clear through to the finish of the shot. If you fall forward or away in your follow-through you can be sure you haven't made the best possible shot, regardless of where the ball goes.

Now your right arm swings all the way around fully outstretched.

Note how the arms seem to be almost flying out of their sockets. They can talk all they want about the follow-through not being an important part of the stroke, but when your follow-through naturally takes your club head after the ball you can be sure that you've got power and direction.

Now the wrists begin to turn over because the arms have reached the limit of possible stretch after the shot. In being carried around by momentum, they make every element of the swing coordinate properly. Note how the club head is finishing high.

Be sure your follow-through is an integral part of your swing and not merely added to it.

55

The Mashie

The most versatile club in the average player's bag is the mashie, when it's allowed to do its work without being handicapped by a tendency to scoop the ball. Hit down at it.

The ball is played a few inches back of a line even with the left heel; not as far back as shown in these pictures. These pictures were taken from about even with my right shoulder to get in more details of knee, shoulder, and hand action.

See how the hands are kept low. Don't try to lift the club. The angles of club lofts are figured to get the ball up off the ground, if you will let them function naturally. Watch the hip position with respect to the light triangle in the background.

The Mashie

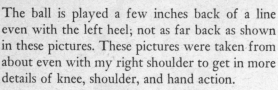

Note that there has been no rolling over of the right arm. The line of the shoulders is almost at right angles to the line of intended flight. See that reach with the left arm; it's straight but it isn't tense.

Watch how the position from the hips down is the same in this illustration and the next one. The action from this point to the top of the swing consists of bringing the hands up to the highest reach permitted by the straight left arm and by cocking the wrists.

58

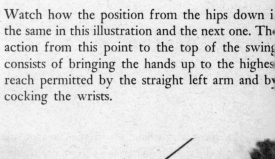

If you will keep your knees on a fairly level plane, instead of dipping the left knee, you'll be far more certain of a correct pivot. The impetus for the pivot feels like it comes from inside the left foot, with the left heel being lifted only enough to make action comfortable.

The right leg has straightened and the right hip is being swung out of the way, so the backswing can proceed smoothly with the left arm straight and the right elbow kept fairly close to the body. The wrists are cocking.

This is the top of the mashie swing. Note that the club's shaft is level with the ground and that the head still is over the ball, just as it was in the addressing. You must feel firmly balanced but not locked, at this point. The grip must be firm but flexible here.

See how the shoulders have turned even though the club hasn't changed position from the previous illustration. The left knee has started toward its eventual straight position.

59

The left foot has come down flat on the ground. There is a feeling of squatting that comes from a change from a fairly flat to an upright arc of the swing. That "sitting down" to the ball keeps the body from getting so stiff it interferes with a free swing.

See how the left side is beginning to feel firm and get anchored to allow a tremendous hit with the hands without jerking the player off balance. This body change must be made without letting the right elbow get far away from the body.

Compare this picture with an illustration of a wood coming into contact with the ball. Then you will see how the mashie shot is more upright, with a snap down into the ball and dependence on the loft of the club to make the ball rise in its correct trajectory.

See the divot flying out behind the club head. This means that the ball was hit a descending blow and that the club was carried on through with the grip being firm enough to make a clean slash of the sod without the wrists being rolled over or the arms slowed up with a jerk.

60

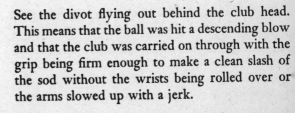

Note that the wrists are in the same position as they were at the top of the swing. The right knee is starting to straighten so the legs, at the moment of impact, will be a firm foundation for the body, arms, and hands performance.

Right here you will see how the wrists are acting at the beginning of a whipping motion. From this point on through the ball, there should be feeling that the wrists are uncocking with a snap at the ends of straight arms.

Again the club head reaches after the ball and the right arm is as straight in the follow-through as the left one was in the backswing. When you get those arms working correctly, with the elbows held almost the same distance apart throughout the swing, you cure a lot of troubles.

See how the left side moves out of the way quickly. The feet are closer together in a mashie shot than with longer irons or woods, hence it should be easier for you to keep to the path of the swing instead of trying to do tricks with your knees.

Finishing this way brings considerable relaxation of the right side.

Just let the hands complete the fling of the club, and if you've been properly balanced and your grip is right you'll finish the shot smoothly and firmly.

Don't "loop" the club head at the finish of the swing.

Let your straight right arm keep the club swinging in a wide arc away from your body.

Note how closely to the body the hands are held. The sole of the club is flat on the ground. Your eyes, hands, and toes are in the same line. Knees are slightly bent.

The right side is being slid back and around, out of the way. The club head is being swung by the arms, and not lifted by the wrists. The shoulders and arms are being moved around by foot, leg, and knee action.

Mashie Shot SIDE VIEW

See at the top of the backswing how the hands are under the club, and because the grip is right there hasn't been any loosening of control of the club. You're ready to pull down with your left arm.

A decided pull with the left arm has brought the right elbow in closer to the body. Note how swiftly the hips are getting into a line with the hole, compared with slow change in shaft position.

64

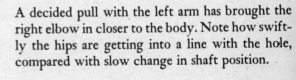

Watch the left knee with respect to the patch of light ahead of it. The knee doesn't dip. The right leg is straightening and the hips are swinging around. Wrist cocking begins slowly here.

Now the wrists are beginning to cock rapidly. At this point you should be looking over your left shoulder at the ball so that you may feel your left shoulder touch your chin.

Now the left foot has come down flat on the ground and is set for allowing the left arm and shoulder to work from a steady axis in getting the club head on the right track back to the ball.

From this point on to the farthest out point of the follow-through, watch how the right arm straightens out. See how the left leg works now, just about as the right one did in the backswing.

Here the wrists start to uncock with all the limberness and speed that can be attained with the proper grip. Watch the hips lift a little and note how the club comes from inside the line of flight to the ball.

Observe that the hands are low and how the club head is going down below the ball. Note how close the right elbow is to the body. The left leg is braced so the power for hitting has a solid anchorage.

The right shoulder action in this follow-through shows you what happens when you correctly hit down at, and through, a mashie shot instead of trying to scoop it up.

The club head has pulled the hands and arms well around in a wide arc.

The hands go through after the ball. You can see that by watching how the right arm is straight and brings the right shoulder down rather than around on a horizontal plane.

Your weight is well on your left foot here, and you hit up against your left hip.

This shot ends with weight on left leg and right side of body and right leg released.

The Short Irons

When to Use Pitching Clubs

THE PITCH SHOT is probably the most spectacular in golf. I know of no other shot that gives me more thrill than to spank a high rising shot and see its backspin halt the ball near the hole. Pitching is invaluable to good scoring, for it is the pitch laid in the vicinity of the flag that affords the player the opportunity to birdie the hole.

The pitching clubs are those graduated from the mashie to the niblick. The shafts are of different lengths. The heads have a varying degree of loft (much more than the longer irons), enabling the player to impart more backspin to the ball. The player will find them easier to play, for, as already stated, in long iron play, as the golfer stands closer to the ball, the stroke becomes rounder and is more accurately made.

The stance for these pitching clubs gets narrower and more open as the shorter sticks are used. It is closer to the ball until the use of the putter brings the player's head directly over the ball. If the player will remember this, he will have little trouble with pitching clubs.

Since little pivot is used, control of the club must be in the hands and arms. Never reach for the ball when playing this shot.

It is not necessary to take a long swing. A little practice with these clubs, starting fifty yards from the green and working back, will soon give the player the range for each club, and an idea as to the length of backswing necessary for the needed distance.

ONE MIGHT CALL these clubs the trouble clubs. They are used in the rough when a bad lie presents itself and it is necessary to get the ball out of sand. When the ball lies close to the green, but has found a shaggy lie, they fill the bill. A chip cannot be made out of long grass.

If the ball requires extraction from heavy rough, you can bank on a well-lofted club to do the job. The player will be wise, if he selects a more lofted club when the lie is heavy, and attempts to cut under the ball. There will be little chance for applying backspin, so don't attempt to hold the green with this shot. Allow for a good margin of run.

70

When a bunker lies in the way, the pitch is the shot to use. Golfers often use the mashie or mashie-niblick on this shot, but when a shorter distance makes a crisp firm shot with these clubs impossible, the niblick is used. There is a distinct advantage in playing a longer approach, for the ball can be firmly hit and a full swing taken. However, it is sometimes necessary to play half shots and three-quarter shots. Under 120 yards, at which point the full niblick is used, the golfer must depend on his ability in varying the stroke so that it will give the desired effect. The ball should be hit firmly, yet must not over-run the green. To accomplish this, move the hands down the leather as the shot becomes shorter.

Greens are built for pitching. They are watered and are softer than the surrounding area. But if they are hard and fast, sometimes it is impossible to hold them, no matter how much backspin is applied. It is then better to use a pitch-and-run shot, aiming at a spot in front of the green and letting the ball run up to the hole. The shot is played with a club with less loft than would normally be called for.

There will be times when the golfer will have to pitch over a trap, and the distance will be so short that the full-hit backspin shot cannot be used; neither can he run the ball through the trap. A niblick should be used and a slice spin be added to make the ball stop with the least run. Lay the face of the club back a little on this shot. A great fault here is indecision — don't baby the shot or "wish" the ball up to the hole.

Set your weight evenly on both feet. The short iron shots, being strokes with comparatively little body turn, need steady arm action.

No wrists in the shot yet. The straight left arm swings the club back easily, smoothly. Both feet are on the ground throughout the backswing.

The Short Irons

You get all the stretch you can with the left arm in the short iron shots, just the same as you do with the longer iron and wood shots.

See how there's very little body action in the three pictures showing the uppermost part of the swing. It's wrist action here.

See how the right elbow stays in close. About when the shaft points at your right pocket, begin to cock your wrists.

Note there's been very little action of the left knee. The short iron swings are very upright, but must be made inside the line of flight.

See how the wrists hinge without any rolling action of the arm to take the club face out of its proper facing.

The left shoulder starts to move away from the chin. Note that the left foot is flat and firm on the ground.

73

By keeping the body action at a minimum the short iron swing is kept upright, and the loft of the clubs is correctly employed.

Here the left leg begins to brace, smoothly, while the left shoulder is bringing the club down to the ball. Wrists are not uncocked.

Note that the left shoulder has not been lifted from the time in the preceding picture when the wrists began to uncock. Stay down to the ball.

74

See that the same firm left side has been maintained to hit against. The turf has been hit after the ball. The down blow raises the ball.

Note there's no evidence of tensity, even though the short iron shots often are recovery shots. The three-quarter swing must not be rushed.

Now the wrists begin to uncock. It's from this point down to the ball that the snap comes for power.

The right side relaxes in order that the follow-through will be smooth and full, and that the factor of precision be kept.

Now the arms and wrists are rolling because the body is turning square to the hole. Note how full arm leverage is used to the end.

75

If you have hit down on the ball properly, the ball will have plenty of backspin.

Keep hitting the short iron shot. If you haven't quit on the shot you'll have a full follow-through.

Practice this shot a lot. Expertness with your short irons will save you many strokes.

As in other shots, finish this swing with a firm grip on the club.

Due to the lie of the club and length of shaft you have to bend over more than with longer club shots. Get your head almost over the ball.

Observe how far inside the line of flight the club head comes without any action of the wrists in lifting the club. The feet are firm.

Short Iron Shot SIDE VIEW

The action is similar to that of coiling a spring; you wind up from the hips until your shoulders and wrists get the club back.

78

Now the wrists are cocked so the club is about at a 45 degree angle with the ground. Three-quarters of a swing is all you need in this.

Watch the shoulders and the wrists start to do the work at this point. There's not much knee-action in the short iron swing.

The straight left arm is the main feature of control of the shot from this point back and down, but the right elbow shouldn't stray.

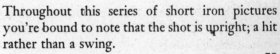

The "sitting down" motion is less pronounced in the short iron shots, but it still is an element in getting punch into the blow.

Throughout this series of short iron pictures you're bound to note that the shot is upright; a hit rather than a swing.

79

Observe how the right arm is straightening even though it continues to be held close to the body. The shoulders are working strongly.

Now the wrists have begun to straighten out so both arms and wrists will be parallel to the club grip when the ball is hit.

Watch the right arm show its place in putting power into the shot. The left is virtually an extension of the club shaft.

A complete follow-through is a sign that the shot has been hit crisply. You have to hit short irons firmly; the loft kills distance.

Get the left side out of the way so the ball can be hit sharply without any interference from the body.

See how the ball has jumped up quickly, although club head has just reached the grass level after hitting down and is taking a divot.

There's no speed in lifting the head in the follow-through because it comes up naturally, and at the right time in response to the proper arm and shoulder action.

81

The Explosion Shot

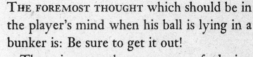

THE FOREMOST THOUGHT which should be in the player's mind when his ball is lying in a bunker is: Be sure to get it out!

There is more than one way of playing recovery shots, but if the trap is deep, if the ball is buried or has found a heel print, methods other than the explosion shot should be disregarded. It is true that the cut shot can be used under similar circumstances, but for safety, the explosion is the shot for the average player.

This shot is mainly used when the ball is to be placed from the trap onto the green, or from a trap close to the green. It is not used when the player requires distance.

First of all, anchor your feet firmly in the sand. Stand well over the ball.

Grip the club low and not at the top of th leather. Swing the club back with a straight lef arm and firm wrists.

The Explosion Shot

From this point on to the top of the swing the action is mostly with the wrists, as you'll note from the shoulder positions.

By keeping the left arm extended you protec yourself against an inclination to try to scoop th ball up, or to hurry and jerk the shot.

Note that the ball is played off the left foot and that the stance is open, with the left foot drawn away from the intended line of flight.

The head must not move, and there's comparatively little leg action, because this is an exceedingly upright swing.

Watch the wrists cock, and see in this picture how the right hand indicates that the face of the club has been "opened" somewhat.

There's the usual very slight pause of all good swings that you'll note at the top of this sand niblick swing.

Observe how the club is hammered down with the shoulders and wrists until the club head digs into the sand well behind the ball. The distance the sand is hit behind the ball determines the length of the shot; however you must judge the firmness and texture of the sand, which you can do when you wiggle your feet around getting a

firm stance. The same straight left on the backswing, with the right elbow in, and the transfer to the straight right in the follow-through, takes place in this shot, as it does in other iron and wood shots.

In the explosion shots the follow-through is highly important. If you get into your mind that you are going through after the shot, you will really hit into it instead of letting the first contact with the sand stop your blow and diminish the effect on the ball.

The Explosion Shot SIDE VIEW

Note how the face of the club is laid back so it will have its greatest power from below when coming into the sand back and under the ball.

The explosion shot is one in which the club head is swung outside the line of intended flight and away from the body. This puts "cut" on the ball and stops it quickly after it lights.

In the explosion shots, come back with a bit more than a three-quarter swing, but don't be afraid to hit the ball. There is not much leg action. The feet, of course, stay firm in the sand. The straight left arm is highly important because it gives you the arc on the ball that otherwise would be hard to get when your club head is not permitted to

touch the ground, as the rules of golf apply to hazards. The left arm and the wrists play the greater part of this shot. The right arm, when its elbow is held close to the body, straightens out automatically when the proper spot in the downswing is reached.

The weight shifts from the right leg to the left one as the club comes down to the ball. Note how the swift action of the wrists near the bottom of the swing bring the face of the club in and across the ball, which normally would impart a slice to the ball.

However, the effect is smothered by the sand that's between the club face and the ball, and the actual result is to pop the ball up into the air and make it fall dead.
Seldom does the average player make consistently satisfactory recovery shots because

he's afraid to hit at the ball hard enough automatically to get a full, firm follow-through. This is no shot to chop and quit on; your excess of power — if you have any — will be safely absorbed by the sand.

The Putt

PUTTING is one department of the game
the player should and can more easily
round into shape. He can get it down to
par figures more quickly than any other
division of the game. Par allows thirty-six
strokes on the putting surface per round,
two on each hole.

It is on the greens that the final result
of the hole is determined. It is the pay-off
spot. Here a player can pick up a stroke
that has been lost in playing from tee to
green. But a stroke lost on the green is
lost forever. There is nothing to make up
after the first putt has been missed.

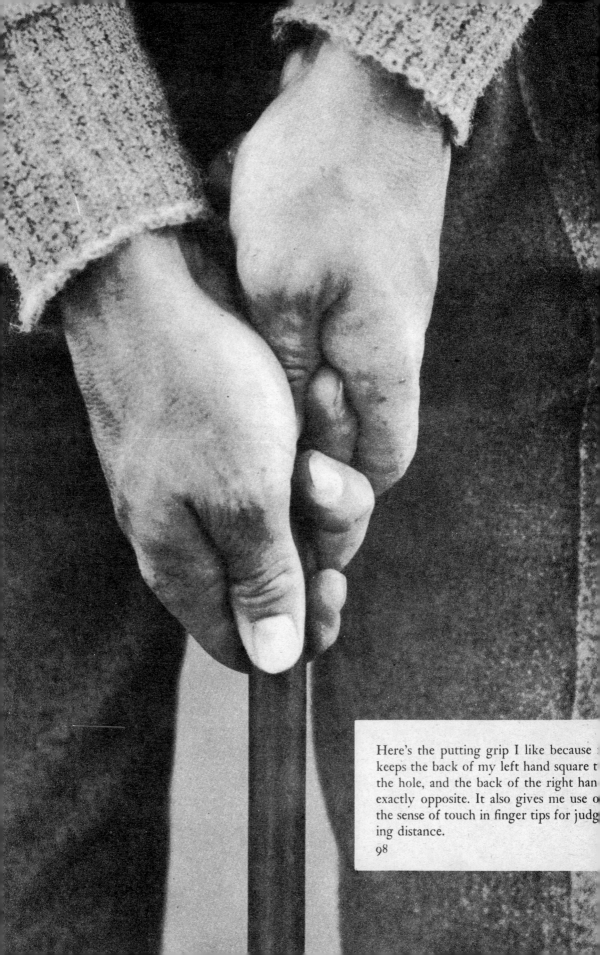

Here's the putting grip I like because
keeps the back of my left hand square t
the hole, and the back of the right han
exactly opposite. It also gives me use o
the sense of touch in finger tips for judg
ing distance.

98

Concentrate, Have Confidence, and Relax

AFTER THE PLAYER has learned the fundamental of the putting stroke, there are three important factors he should master — concentration, confidence, and relaxation.

Concentration is the most important, for the other two factors depend to a great extent on it. But just what concentration is, and how to achieve and put this faculty into use, is hard for the golfer to assimilate. Concentration is the faculty of being able to eliminate everything from the mind except the performance of the fundamental parts of the stroke — one at a time. This includes selecting the proper line to the hole, the proper stance and grip, and estimating correctly the length of the backswing. Having done these, the player now has confidence. This confidence is a self-assurance that the fundamentals have been correctly executed, so that the golfer needs only to think of the final act of swinging the putter — excluding all other thoughts from his mind.

With confidence, the player relaxes — and relaxation is conducive to good golf. It is hard to relax if one lacks confidence. When the player is not sure that he has correctly judged the line to the hole, or is worrying about his grip, he cannot stroke the ball smoothly. He is certain to attempt a last-second alteration of the stroke, upsetting the smooth, rhythmic swing.

Since the putting stroke depends so much on these three important factors, the golfer should experiment with his stance and stroke until he has found the one that is most comfortable; that is, the one, the fundamentals of which he will find easier to concentrate on, which gives him the confidence that results in relaxation.

The Putt

In putting get the line you want by coming up to the ball from the back, and studying the route. Then be sure that your putter blade is flat on the ground and squarely across the line so you can hit the ball firmly in the middle of the blade. That's the purpose for which your putter was designed. Get your left eye (if that's your master eye)

right over the ball. Have both toes even on a line parallel with that which you want the ball to travel when it leaves the club.

Hold your hands in close.

Putt the ball almost off the left toe, and keep the putter blade low to the ground. Have the blade stay square across the line as long as you can, comfortably, on the back-swing.

On a fast downhill putt, hold the club a bit looser than when you have to make an uphill putt.

The Putt FRONT VIEW

Observe how the left eye, the hands, and the ball are practically in a straight line. The knees are relaxed, but the body is held motionless and without tensity. The wrists do the work as you may observe from the spot of light near the left elbow. See how

easily, but firmly, the left arm is resting on the left leg.

When the putt is hit the left forearm slides gently and in a straight path, and the right hand follows with both hands in such position that, if they were opened, they would be squarely together. The head is held steady until well after the ball is hit. At no time is there body action in the putt.

*Professional Tips
on How to Improve Your Score*

Addressing the Ball

It is hard to keep one's balance when reaching for the ball . . . stand almost erect, letting the arms drop naturally from the shoulders.

SINCE THE POSITION at impact is similar to that taken at the start of the backswing it is important that the body and its parts are in the correct position before any action takes place. The player must be properly set, to get a good start toward a successful shot.

The distance one stands from the ball should be given consideration. A stance too far away flattens the swinging arc, requiring extreme finesse to have the club-head properly meet the ball square to the line. The position of the feet from the ball should vary according to the height and build of the individual. This is where the taller players have a slight advantage over the shorter ones; they can stand closer to the ball. This enables them to swing the club in a rounder, or more close to the vertical, arc, and greater accuracy is attained.

The feet should be comfortable. A good stance has the feet apart about the width of the shoulders. The weight should be evenly divided.

Stand fairly erect. Reaching must be avoided if balance throughout the swing is to be maintained. The arms and club should not form a straight line, but an angle. A good position at address has the arms falling naturally from the shoulders with the hands neither too close nor stretched out too far.

Since the stroke for the irons necessitates a downward blow, the swing is more upright, and the clubhead is brought down more abruptly on the ball. Move the feet closer together as the shorter clubs are used.

The Pivot

Shift the weight to the right foot in the backswing and turn the right hip to allow the hands to swing past.

THE PIVOT is probably the least understood of all golf actions. It is not just the twisting of the waist; neither is it the action of dropping the left shoulder toward the ball, as the duffer does.

Pivoting is the swinging of the club to the top of the backswing in a wide arc, with the left foot, knee, hip, and shoulder turning toward the right.

It is through this turning of the hips and shoulders that some golfers outdrive others who have more strength and weight.

Harry Vardon once said: "Golfers find it a very trying matter to turn at the waist, more particularly if they have a lot of waist to turn. But they must learn to do so if they would acquire any proficiency at all; it is the only way to success at golf."

A turn of the body is necessary, because there is no other way to get into position to hit the ball with power and force, yet with ease and rhythm. The pivot places the body behind the swing and gives freedom to the hands, wrists, and arms to do their part of the job. The turn of the body should be made naturally and comfortably, letting the hands swing fairly close to the body.

When the left shoulder drops and the golfer fails to complete the prior pivot, the right shoulder is swung too low in the downswing and the clubhead hits the ground. This fault can be traced to failure of the golfer to shift his weight to the right leg in the backswing.

The pivot isn't an artificial action; it is a natural turn of the body. Without holding a club, stand upright and turn the shoulders and hips from left to right and back again. This is simply the pivot action. Notice that in order to get the shoulders at right angles to the starting position, the left knee bends, and the left heel leaves the ground.

Straight Left Arm

A STRAIGHT LEFT ARM is not essential to good golf, but it is good form, and is conducive to a good game. Many fine golfers bend the left arm slightly at the top of the backswing, but early in the downswing, it is straightened so that at impact it is in a position that forms a straight line from the clubhead to the left shoulder.

Any excessive bend in the left arm destroys a feeling of power and force in the wrists. And don't forget, a straight left arm does not mean that it must be stiff; it should be only comfortably straight.

The left arm acts as a measuring stick to gauge correctly the distance to the ball. No measure can be accurately made unless the tape is tight — remember, a straight line is the shortest distance between two points, and not around a bent arm.

The left arm connects the club to the left shoulder, which is the hub of the swing. By keeping it straight, the swinging arc is lengthened, enabling the golfer to get a longer sweep at the ball.

One point to concentrate on is to see that the left arm is absolutely straight at impact. A bend at this position in the swing can only lead to heeling, topping, or missing the ball entirely, or to many other faults that result from the clubhead traveling beyond or inside the line of flight.

The extended left arm is also an aid to firmness, which is necessary in the swing.

The Follow Through and the Finish

THE FOLLOW THROUGH plays just as important a part in golf as it does in other sports. It results in an easy, rhythmical swing that is so all important to good golf. It is that part of the swing in which the clubhead travels for a few inches low and close to the ground after the ball is struck. If the player gives this part of the stroke a little thought, he will be aided in correctly executing those parts of the swing that precede it.

Maybe you are one of those golfers who say, "Why bother with that part of the swing that takes place after the ball is struck? Nothing can be done to alter the ball's flight after it has been sent on its way."

This is a fair question. It is answered by the following fact. By trying to make the clubhead follow out after the ball, the golfer will find that the hit has been from the inside. The left arm has stayed firm, and the hands have been kept in the correct path.

After the follow through takes place — but not before — the head may be raised. Now the player is ready for the finish of the stroke. The follow through continues with the right arm straight and the right knee bent. The body turns until the golfer faces the hole. At the finish, the right arm is fairly straight, and the wrists break. The finish should closely resemble the top of the backswing, but in reverse.

Timing

IT IS AN ODD FACT, but true, that no two golfers swing alike. This is remarkable, considering the number of fine professionals and amateurs. Yet all good golfers, through experience and practice, have developed timing suited to the movements of their individual swing. Timing is the co-ordination of all actions into one continuous, easy, flowing movement. This is the secret of the long accurate hitter.

To develop timing, the player must avoid tension and relax. The tighter the tension, the simpler it is to forget golf's basic fundamentals on which timing and rhythm of the swing depend.

A baseball pitcher cannot show his usual speed and control in throwing, if he jerks his arm back quickly. Whenever possible, he takes a slow, easy windup, and then puts his full power into the throw. Neither can the golfer control the club by quickly raising and lowering the clubhead. He must start slowly and gradually accelerate in the downswing so that the clubhead is traveling at its greatest speed at impact.

When you have reason to believe your timing is off, slow down the backstroke. Arrest the action at the start of the swing by pushing the club back slowly with the left hand. Do not pick it up in a hurry, tossing it over your shoulder.

Wait for the backswing to be completed before starting the club down, and avoid rushing the right shoulder around before the clubhead has reached the hitting area. Lead the club down with the left hand and arm so that the clubhead will be brought around on an inside arc.

Turning the body too quickly in the downswing can only result in a badly timed shot. This is called hitting too soon. Eagerness to hit hard is the common fault of the ordinary player. The experts delay the complete turn of the body toward the hole to allow the hands and arms to come through. Better control and distance will be obtained if the player will keep his body out of the swing until he wants the final punch, co-ordinating with the wrists, arms, and hands. However, don't be misled by thinking that the body stays out of the shot entirely. Good timing necessitates the natural turn of the body on both the backswing and the downswing.

Backswing

Start the club back with a push from the left side through the left hand and arm.

IF THE GOLFER wishes to achieve a certain amount of success and desires to lower his score, he should pay particular attention to the backswing. This highly important item will not take care of itself, as so many mediocre golfers think. These players wonder what is wrong when scores mount and shots go astray. It would be to their advantage to concentrate on executing a good backswing, and let the downswing take care of itself. Such thoughts as power needed in the downswing to make the ball travel a needed distance down the fairway should be excluded from their minds.

If the backswing is not properly performed, there can be little hope for a successful downswing. The player must be in a good position to accomplish the hitting part of the stroke.

Get set mentally before starting any motion. Think in terms of smoothness, excluding the desire to rush and hurry. Remember, one can, and should, spend twice as much time on the backswing as on the downswing.

After mental assurance is gained, the golfer should think of starting the club back with a push from the left side through the left hand and arm as the body turns. The club will be the last thing to move and will be dragged away from the ball, lagging behind the hands. This start will help toward a correct pivot. Allow the right hip to turn so that it will not block the hands and arms. The hips and shoulders should turn until the back of the player is presented to the hole.

Guard against breaking the wrists too quickly, for such action will hinder the success of the pivot and the top of the swing will be reached before the pivot is completed. Let the wrists be cocked when the upper part of the backswing is reached. If the player will start the club back low and close to the ground, controlled by the left hand, breaking of the wrists too soon will be avoided.

Action of Hands and Arms

THE LEFT HAND is responsible for maintaining the correct position of the clubhead throughout the swing. Therefore, a secure grip must be maintained at all times. But golf is not just a left-handed game. The right also should have a reasonably secure hold on the club, for it plays its part in the downswing when it whips the club through the hitting region.

The right hand must not be allowed to overpower the left, for an overpowering right hand turns the clubface out of position, often cutting across the line of flight. Let the left hand and arm dominate the backswing and the downswing.

Do not grip too fiercely. The grip must be firm, but when the fingers grip too tightly, tension may spread to all parts of the body. Tight fingers cause the muscles of the arms to tighten. This is bound to result in a jerky swing.

To loosen the muscles of the hands and forearms, a waggle is recommended. A practice swing is also a good way to get properly set for the swing.

Instructors advise their pupils to start the downswing slowly. The reason for this is to guard against the arms swinging too swiftly toward the objective. Such action causes one to force or press the shot. When the golfer begins to press, the arms are traveling so fast the body cannot keep pace. Thus the stroke is made with the arms alone, and power is lost. Speed of the arms should be gradually increased. The climax comes with the forward snap of the wrists.

Analyze Your Grip

"V's" formed should point over the right shoulder.

WHETHER THE GOLFER uses the interlocking, the old-fashioned baseball, or the popular overlapping or Vardon grip, the left hand should be turned over the shaft. Analyzing the grip will show that this assists one in keeping a straight left arm by slightly increasing the tension of the left elbow, preventing it from crumbling at impact.

A firmer grip on the club is advised by the experts for iron play. It is necessary to carry the clubhead through. Don't confuse this with tightening of the wrists. This must be avoided at all times.

In a sand trap or heavy rough, the firm grip is of utmost importance, for it is sometimes necessary literally to plow through the grass or sand to get the ball out. Grasp the club firmly enough so that any obstruction will not turn the club in your hands. If this happens, the clubface will be presented to the ball at an incorrect angle.

While on the subject of the grip, let me warn you about the right hand. Faulty placement of it can be the direct cause for the quick-diving smothered shot, or the hooked iron. When the right hand is placed too far under the shaft, a rolling action of the wrists takes place, which results in turning the right hand over the left. This closes the face of the clubhead or hoods the club just before impact, resulting in the diving hook.

Practice

THE PRACTICE TEE is the place to make corrections. Even professionals practice as much as they play. Experimenting when the chips are down might be disastrous.

But if you find your No. 5 iron is not working properly, do not rush to the practice tee and begin hitting No. 5 iron shots. First get the advice of your pro, find the fault, and then proceed to correct it. Just hitting shots, hoping the stroke will correct itself, is useless. You then are inclined to repeat the error over and over again.

It is a good idea to practice before a round of golf. A fifteen-minute warmup will help your game considerably. But do not practice with one club too long, for when interest wanes, practice is useless. The player then gets careless with the stroke and often bad hits are formed.

Practice loosens muscles that have been more or less idle and which will be used during a round. Arm, shoulder, and back muscles are called on to do work to which they are unaccustomed. Practice loosens the wrists, the action of which is essential to good golf.

Start practice by hitting a few putts. Then work up to the longer clubs.

A fine way to start practice with the irons is to start pitching at a distance of about twenty-five yards from the green. If, after a dozen shots, you are satisfied with the results, move back another twenty-five yards. If this stroke also clicks move back another twenty-five yards, and so on. In this manner you are bound to find the spot at which your shots may not be working so well, and so be able to correct your swing. This method also gradually loosens the muscles used in the longer strokes without putting them to too great a strain at once.

Causes for Topped Shots

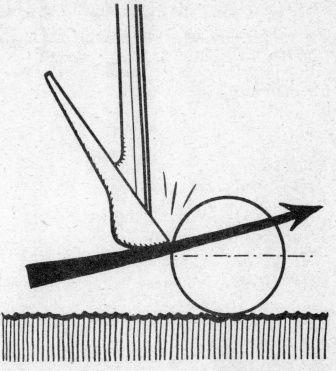

Topped shot results when ascending clubhead hits ball above center.

TOPPING A SHOT is aggravating, and one topped shot is apt to ruin the complacency and rhythm of all but the most composed golfers.

This annoying accident is mainly caused by the golfer trying to lift the ball into the air with a body action, or by a flick of the wrists. When the golfer tries to get the ball into the air in this manner, he fails to shift the weight onto the left leg, keeps too much on the right, and the result is that the lowest point in the swinging arc is moved backward.

A topped ball is seldom hit on top, as the duffer imagines. It actually is hit above center after the clubhead has reached the lowest point in the downswing and has begun to ascend.

Another cause for a topped shot is looking up or lifting the head before impact. This action draws the clubhead out of its intended path. Also responsible for a "top," is a failure to pivot. This fault lets the right shoulder drop in the down-swing. When this happens, the chances are that the clubhead will hit the ground before the ball is topped. Still another cause for this annoyance is the tendency to play the ball too far advanced. It then can only be hit an upward blow, and you will be lucky if the ball is hit cleanly if played from such a position.

Learn the fundamentals of the swing, practice them diligently, and your topping will stop.

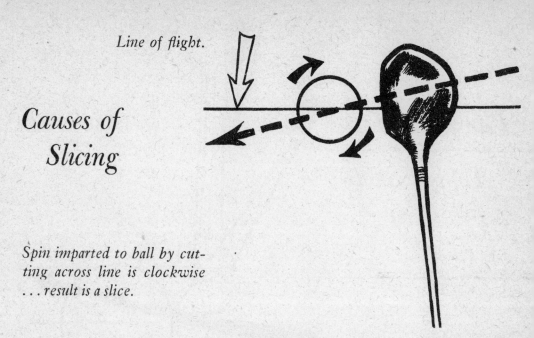

Line of flight.

Causes of Slicing

*Spin imparted to ball by cutting across line is clockwise
...result is a slice.*

EXPERTS SELDOM SLICE, because their swing has been built with the idea of hooking the ball. The average golfer, however, still in the early stages of building his game, finds the slice a troubling factor, and is bewildered and helpless when it comes to correcting it.

Many faults can creep into the swing to cause the ball to be hit in a disgusting, though graceful arc into the rough to the right of the fairway. The main reason however is that the face of the clubhead has been drawn across the ball. This means that the clubhead has been caused to travel in a path that cuts across the line of flight from the outside.

But one must go farther back in the swing to find the sources for this cut across the ball. Too wide a stance is one. Lack of proper control by the left hand is another. When the left hand quits, there is no guiding factor to hold the clubhead along the line of flight, and it is drawn sharply in toward the left side.

Chronic slicers get the hands and body into the stroke too soon. In their anxiety to hit, the hands and body lead the clubhead at impact. When the clubhead is allowed to drag behind, the clubface strikes the ball while at a distinct angle, with the heel ahead of the toe or with an open face.

A similar position of the clubface may be traced to the bend or collapse of the left arm or the lack of wrist snap, at or just before impact.

If slicing is to be cured, check on these points: see that the clubhead is started back inside the line; that the left side is completing the turn, with the weight shifted against the right leg; that the left hand and arm are dominating the backswing and the start of the downswing; and that the stance is not that for the intentional slice which hinders a complete pivot.

Playing in the Wind

THERE ARE FEW PLAYERS who enjoy a round of golf on a windy day. Wind not only affects the flight of the ball, but plays havoc with the player's morale.

The ball must be more accurately hit when playing in a gale; therefore the first thing to do is shorten the backswing and hit less viciously. A shorter swing is more compact, affords the player better balance, and he is less likely to err. Do not fight the wind. It is an invisible, unbeatable opponent.

Wind magnifies mistakes, and shots that would look as if perfectly played on a calm day, are completely carried away.

A low trajectory shot is the one desired in iron play. Use a club with less loft, and play a half-iron shot. The ball will be lower and, although it may run more than a highly hit approach, direction, the thing to be achieved, is the result.

Try teeing the ball a little lower for the wood shots. Through the fairway, when the lie is good, a driver often should be the club selected in preference to the brassie.

If the wind is blowing from left to right, don't aggravate a condition by allowing for the wind to swing the ball back to the middle of the fairway. The golfer then unconsciously assumes a stance of that for the intentional slice. A ball hit in this manner slices more than ever. The idea is to play for a slight draw. This can be accomplished by turning the left wrist more over the shaft, or closing the stance slightly so that the hit from the inside is accentuated. The reverse holds true if the wind is blowing from right to left. Open the stance and hit with the clubhead slightly open.

When shooting directly into the wind off the tee, many golfers employ what is known as the "knock down shot." They play the ball more toward the right foot and connect with a descending stroke. This shot has a low start, a quick rise, and, due to the backspin, stops almost instantly upon striking the ground. It is a good one to use for second shots to the green, but has little value as a distance-getter. The best distance-getter is the ball, whether playing in the wind or not, that is struck squarely in the back. Let it take its normal trajectory and you will find it a better boring ball than one hit in the other manner.

Top of the Backswing

A pause at the top of the backswing will check the desire to kill the ball.

IF THE ACTIONS of the backstroke have been made correctly, the golfer will feel a pull at the left shoulder with the right arm and shoulder relaxed. The left side will be taut, for it will start the action back toward the ball.

If the right side is in control here, there is an irresistible desire to hit from this position, with a tendency to turn the shoulders as soon as the downswing is started. Therefore, be sure control is in the left hand.

Here the greater portion of the weight should have been shifted to the right foot. If it has not, the backswing has been checked and is working against a resisting force. The shoulders then cannot swing around, and the hips bend in a sideward action to the left rather than turning in a rotating manner toward the right.

At the top of the backswing, the grip on the shaft must be firm. Often golfers open the hands here, with the result that the grip is altered in the downswing. Then when contact with the ball is made, the grip is not the same as it was at address.

Studying the Putt

THE PUTTER is probably the most neglected club in the bag. It is hard to make the golfer realize the value of the putt. He figures that par allows him 36 putts on the carpet, and any figure in that vicinity is satisfactory and good putting. It isn't good putting and shouldn't be satisfactory to any golfer. It is on the greens that the golfer should give Old Man Par a licking.

118

If the player is to improve in this department, there are things he should do besides executing the fundamentals described elsewhere on these pages. Mental condition has a great bearing on results. Worries over a past score, a business deal back in town, or other personal problems will be of no help. These worries will affect putting more than any other part of the game. This is the delicate part of the game, and a cool head is mandatory. Put all thoughts out of your mind but that one of sending the ball to the bottom of the cup.

There are also things the golfer should do before he addresses the ball. He should study the green, surveying the line to the hole. Determine the roll of the green. Study the grass, noting whether it grows in a certain way; that is, if the blades all seem to lean in one direction. They will have a decided effect on the path of the ball, pushing it in the direction they are leaning. This is important when playing a rolling green. Against the grass grain, the golfer should allow less burrow. With the grain, the ball will break quicker. Putting against the grain requires a harder tap than putting with it.

The Importance of a Proper Stance

THE STANCE is the foundation of the swing, but the foundation will crumble and along with it the golfer's game if the placement of the feet is made improperly. Therefore, it is an all-important factor to check the foundation and see that it is in line and that its parts are in the proper place.

The proper stance has the knees slightly bent so that relaxation throughout the swing is maintained. Toes point outward so that tension in the legs is avoided. The feet should not be placed too far apart. Pivoting will then be difficult. It is much easier to complete the pivot if the feet are closer together.

With a wide stance, instead of pivoting naturally, the player is bound to sway in an effort to complete the backswing. It is then impossible to get the body into the stroke, and a shorter shot results. A narrower stance enables the player to impart considerable acceleration to the clubhead with the body turn alone.

Golfers speak of three kinds of stances. The square is the most popular. It has the toes lined up evenly with the line of flight. The open stance, used by many golfers when playing iron shots, has the left foot drawn away from the line of flight. It is a good stance to use when one is over-swinging. The closed stance has the right foot drawn back from the line, and is often used by the golfer who finds it difficult to pivot. It is the stance taken to play the intentional hook.

Whichever stance is used, be sure it is suited to your swing.

Wrists at Top
of Swing

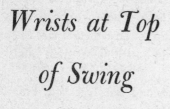

*If these wrinkles do not form
at the top of the backswing
the grip is faulty . . .*

POWER IN THE WRISTS puts power in the golfer's swing, and the cocking of them in the backswing imparts speed and power in the downswing when they are uncocked. If the wrists are not cocked at the top of the swing, the golfer depends on his speed and power to come from the body, and exerts a tremendous effort to attain only a portion of the efficiency attainable in the swing. Without the wrists being cocked, the golfer is very likely to press his swing.

Power behind a carpenter's hammer comes from cocking the wrists, and not from the muscles of his arm. Try swinging a hammer without a cock of the wrist, and note the lack of power in the blow.

Wrists are the hinges of the golf swing, connecting the hands and club with the arms and body. They must work with freedom and ease, and not like the rusty hinge that squeaks and complains under any action. Well-oiled and free, the hinge works smoothly. Avoid a vise-like grip; a firm but easy one frees the wrists of tension. If the wrists lack freedom and ease, the player attempts to make up the loss of power by quickly lunging at the ball in the downswing.

To achieve distance off the tee, it is imperative that the wrists should be cocked and in the correct position at the top of the backswing. Here there should be a distinct bend in the left wrist, so that the hand points inward toward the right shoulder, with the right wrist almost vertical under the shaft.

The golfer might check to see that wrinkles are formed just below the thumb and index finger of the left hand. The grip is faulty if the wrinkles do not appear. The hands have been placed too far under the shaft in gripping at address.

With this imperfection it is impossible to derive maximum power from the wrists, for the hit will be but a backhanded slap by the left wrist. More power is secured by hitting sideways — another reason why the left hand should be turned more over the shaft than under; in other words, good wrist action at the top of the backswing depends on the correct grip.

120

Side Hill Lies

THERE ARE NO OTHER SHOTS in golf that will test the player's skill more than abnormal lies. Side hill lies are bugaboos, and the golfer should know how to play them, for all shots off the fairway are not from level ground.

The golfer often goes about playing from this lie with the idea that, being handicapped, he must give it a bit more effort; rather, he should bear in mind that the stroke should be made with less effort than he is wont to give.

As when playing in a wind, the golfer is tempted to add a bit more power to the stroke and probably presses as a result. The more difficult the lie, the more easily the golfer should go about recovery.

When playing a side hill lie in which the ball rests on the ground in a higher position than the feet, the feeling is always one of cramped conditions. To correct this, the swing is restricted. You have to grip the club a little lower, therefore the arc of swing is shorter. The club feels lighter and a quicker swing is the result. Careful timing of this shot is essential. Guard against falling away from the shot. Keep your head down.

When the ball is lower than the feet, one gets the feeling that the club is too short, and the player may find himself reaching for the ball. Keep the arc of the swing within its limits, and again watch your turning.

Quick Cure for Hooking and Slicing

TWO OF THE MAIN DEFECTS in his game which a golfer should know how to correct quickly are hooking and slicing, those bugaboos which put the player in more hot water and into more difficult lies than probably any other department of the game.

To make the correction, the golfer first must know the cause. Spin is the factor that produces a hooked or sliced shot, and this is imparted to the ball by the clubhead cutting across the ball. A hook is produced by hitting the ball from inside the line of flight out; a slice results from hitting from outside the line of flight in.

Of the two aggravations, slicing is the most common in the swing of the average golfer. One of the most common reasons for a sliced shot is that, when on the tee, determined to avoid a slice, the player will generally try to yank the shot to the left of the fairway. This results in the clubhead being pulled in, cutting across the ball and imparting a slice spin.

Here's how to go about curing your slice — first check the rudiments of your swing, making sure your grip is correct and that your stance is not for the intentional slice, which has the left foot drawn back from the line of flight, which is purposely used to get around obstacles between the golfer and green on occasions. Now attempt to hit the ball to the right of the fairway. This will aid in bringing the clubhead in to the ball more from the inside.

When the player runs into a period of hooking, the hit from the inside has been amplified. The left hand no doubt is throwing the club away from the body and the right elbow is too far from the side of the body in the downswing. This, of course, does not apply to the badly-smothered diving hook that quickly scampers into the rough. This is caused by the hands rolling over, or the right shoulder being higher than the left at impact.

A quick cure for the hook is the reverse action to that which is used to cure a slice — try to hit to the left of the fairway.

The Cut Shot

To stop the ball quickly when playing a shot of 50 yards or less, lay the face of the niblick back.

THE CUT SHOT is one that saves any golfer many strokes. It is used in a situation where the ball needs extraction from heavy grass, or from a trap. Often it is used to pitch the ball onto the green when it is necessary to make the ball stop quickly.

When the normal loft of the club is not sufficient to make the ball rise quickly, this is the shot to use.

Successfully to play this shot out of a sand trap, the ball should be played off the left foot with an open stance. The body should almost be facing the hole.

The club should be laid well back and taken outside the line of flight, cutting across the line in the downswing. Objective of the golfer should be to cut under the ball, slicing a thin cushion of sand between it and the clubhead. Supple wrists are necessary here, as the shot calls for plenty of wrist action.

Here you should be able to differentiate between force and effort. Enough force should be used to cause the club to bite through the sand, but it is not a shot that requires an enormous amount of effort. The moment you think of exerting too much effort, you immediately eliminate the naturalness that should accompany the shot. When the player tries to give the shot all he has — and often more than he has — the backswing is hurried, and a quick lunge at the ball results in an inaccurate, ill-timed blow.

When playing the shot off solid ground, often in a grassy lie, the ball is played more toward the right foot with an open stance. Be sure to hit the ball first, taking a bit of turf with the clubhead after it has made contact with the ball.

Value of Good Form

ONE CAN SOON REALIZE the value of good form if he will take a moment to study its meaning. Good form is the co-ordination of all parts of the swing into continuous rhythmic movement. It cannot be imitated; it must be achieved by constant practice.

Some players attain a certain amount of success without good form, but all good golfers have it. Their styles may vary, but they all have form.

Webster's dictionary defines "form" as "appearance to the eye." If something looks good, it has good form. If a player's swing looks good, he has good form, and you can be sure he has executed the different parts of the swing correctly. Another Webster definition says: "to model by instruction and discipline." Therefore, if the player has learned the fundamentals of the swing from instruction, and if he disciplines his mind to execute them correctly, he cannot help but reach his goal, *Good Form.*

If the swing is to look good, the player must be able to do the thing he wants to in a free and easy manner without strain or tension. Bobby Jones once said, "Good form simply is the means of eliminating waste motion and of exerting, in a useful way, a greater portion of the physical strength which the player possesses."

Trap Shots

Let club enter sand about an inch behind ball.

Low scores are made by saving strokes, and the average player wastes more of them in a trap than any other place on the course. To him, a trip into a bunker is a harrowing experience.

When in a trap, it is important that the player have a proper coordination of mind, muscles, and nerves. This controls perfect timing.

There are four ways of extracting a ball from the sand. They are dependent on the lie, how far the ball is from the pin, whether the sand is wet or dry, how far the ball should be hit, and how much sand it is required to take.

The explosion shot is the safest way out of a bunker. The stance must be firm — so wiggle the feet in the sand until you are well set. The shot is played off the left foot. Stand fairly erect and try a fairly upright swing, brought rather sharply down, driving the clubhead on through just beneath the ball. Let the clubhead enter the sand a few inches behind the ball. In other words, try to hit the sand under the ball, forcing it against the bottom of the ball rather than hitting behind the ball. The latter action drives the sand against the side, circumventing your desire to loft the ball. Properly executed, a quick loft is assured and you will be out in one stroke.

Range can be determined by the amount of sand taken. If it is dry and loose, the hit behind the ball can be farther than if the sand is wet and heavy. Don't let the clubhead strike the ball; the force of the sand under the ball will send it out.

124

Another factor to be sure of is to follow through, and not to let the club quit and stay buried in the sand. You need not fear knocking the ball too far if enough sand is taken.

The cut shot has been explained elsewhere. It is a delicate shot to play out of traps, and one that requires considerable practice.

The chip shot can be employed if the lie is favorable and the ball is not buried. The ball must be hit cleanly. Do not attempt to use this stroke if the bank is steep and the top is covered with overhanging grass.

The putter can also be used to good effect if the trap is shallow.

One of the most common faults of the golfer who finds himself in a bunker is to look up too soon as he makes his recovery shot. Keep the head down and the body relaxed.

If the lie in the trap is good and distance is needed, the shot is played the same as from the fairway. But don't ground the club — it's against the rules.

Backspin or English

THERE ARE TIMES in a round of golf when it is necessary to impart English, or backspin, to the ball so that when it hits the green it will come to a quick stop.

Hitting a shot with backspin is an easy matter if the golfer will get one fact firmly in mind — the ball must be hit a downward blow and be struck before the clubhead bites into the turf.

A backspin shot is not made with a wide stance; rather, it is made with one that is open, heels just a few inches apart. The ball is played off the right foot.

Remembering that your shot must leave the ball nearly dead on the green — keep the left arm straight through the stroke — go into the shot with determination. If correctly made, the hands will finish out in front pointing toward the objective. The length of the backswing varies according to the distance to be carried.

Backspin is not only used when pitching, but is also of great value when correctly applied to the chip shot. When used for chipping, backspin is applied by pinching the ball between the clubface and the ground at impact. This will make the ball take off quickly and travel in a low arc. You may think it has been hit too hard, but watch how it pulls up after hitting the green. It seems to have brakes.

A ball with backspin bores its way and holds its line. That is why experts rely on backspin for accuracy even in high wind.

In connection with backspin, the golfer should know how to apply what is known as "fade" to the ball so that when an opening presents itself to the left of the green he can make the ball travel in from that side. This is done by assuming an open stance and cutting across the intended line of flight as the clubhead comes into the ball.

Recovery Shots

TAKE INVENTORY on the shots wasted in a round, and note how many were caused by failing to recover correctly. The recovery should be made with only one stroke. In other words, when a shot has gone astray, be sure to select a club that will get you out in one stroke and execute it so that no more are needed to get out of trouble.

A little attention and correct thinking can save the golfer from five to ten strokes in a trip around the course. Don't gamble three strokes trying to save one.

Average golfers do not like to practice recovery shots. Seldom do you see any practice from heavy rough, or from a sand trap. Remember, to be able to recover from a bad spot is just as important as avoiding the error that put you there in the first place.

The same distance cannot be made from heavy rough that can be made from a clean lie in the fairway. It is foolish to shoot for the green when it is impossible to reach it. It is better to pitch to the fairway and play the ball from there.

There is little reason for using the cut shot when the maximum distance is required. The cut shot floats in the air, and is used only for short recoveries. To obtain length out of the rough, play the ball more off the right foot and hit with an upright arc, bringing the clubhead down sharply on the ball. No attempt should be made to hit the ball with a sweeping blow, for the long grass will slow up the clubhead.

Sometimes a golfer's sporting blood will entice him to try a shot out of water. It has been done, and is similarly played to the explosion from sand. However, the chances are against you unless part of the ball is lying above the surface of the water. Water bends light rays at crazy angles, and if the ball is completely covered, and fairly deep, it may be a few inches from the spot at which you are looking. When in water, it is safer to take the one-stroke penalty and drop behind the hazard.

Lawson Little once took twelve strokes to recover from water when playing in the Greater Greensboro, N. C. Open of 1938. Ray Ainsley, during the National Open at Cherry Hills, Denver, in 1939, amassed the total of nineteen for a par 4 hole by attempting to play a ball out of water.

The Right Arm and Elbow

Keep right arm and elbow close to side.

To INSURE CONTROL at the top of the backswing, the right elbow must not be allowed to wander too far from the right side. Never should the arm be lifted higher than the shoulder. When it is, the golfer can look for a faulty pivot. If the turn of the body has not been completed, it is impossible to get the club to the horizontal position in the backswing without committing this error.

When this fault takes place, the golfer can be sure that the right hand has played too great a part in the backward movement, and you can look for it to dominate the downswing by hitting as soon as the forward stroke gets under way. A hook or a badly smothered shot can easily result.

When the right arm is kept close, the right hand will not overpower the left.

Discard Wooden Tee on Short Holes

SINCE TURF should be taken when playing an iron shot, it is far better to play from a favorable spot on the teeing surface rather than set the ball up on a wooden peg.

In iron play, the ball must be hit a downward blow; therefore turf must be taken and backspin applied to be accurate. If the ball is teed, it is almost impossible to take turf. The ball slides off the clubface and less backspin is applied than when the ball is pinched between the turf and the clubface.

If a raised ball gives you more confidence, do as other players do — flick up a bit of earth with the toe of the clubhead and rest the ball on top of that.

Speed of Clubhead

*The left arm and club form
a straight line at impact.*

THE LENGTH of a drive depends on the speed of the clubhead. The faster it travels, the farther the ball travels.

The clubhead should be swung as rapidly as is accurately possible, and speed is dependent on correct wrist action.

Most golfers hit too soon; that is, they begin the uncoiling of the wrists long before the hands have moved two-thirds of the way down from the top position. Hitting force then has been expended before the clubhead reaches the ball.

From the cocked position at the top of the backswing, the wrists remain in the same relation to the shaft of the club until half-way through the downswing. Here is little change, except that the forward wrist action of the right hand, which until now has stayed out of the swing, takes place. The hands may then travel only a few inches while the clubhead moves three feet or more. The clubhead now is reaching the maximum speed as the right hand snaps it through the ball.

Viewed from in front of the player, the correct action of the wrists brings the shaft of the club and the left arm in a straight line at impact.

Difference in Wood and Iron Strokes

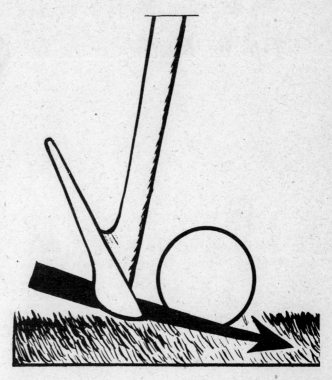

In iron play hit the ball a downward blow . . .

Few GOLFERS who score over 100 for a round realize that there is a distinct difference in the wood shot and that with the iron. They go their merry way swinging both clubs alike.

The arc of the swing in wood play is longer than for the iron. It is essentially a sweep, and has more follow through than that of the iron. It makes less contact with the ground.

Accuracy, not distance, is the aim when playing an iron; hence a shorter backswing. The abbreviated swing requires less pivot, and the stroke is more of a punch or a distinct hit.

The downswing of both strokes is much the same up until the time of contact with the ball. Just before reaching the lowest point in the arc of the downswing, the iron meets the ball in a crisp descending blow, then tears into the turf. In the wood shot, the ball is struck while the clubhead is at the lowest point in the downswing, hitting the ball a sweeping blow.

Tips on Putting

Allow the wrists to work when putting . . . stiffness must be avoided.

TENSION IS A FACTOR that can cause the player to have a bad day on the putting surface. If the muscles of the forearm tighten, the ball is stabbed with a stiff, jerky swing, instead of a free, pendulum action. Allow the wrists to have freedom by loosening the grip on the club.

As in other golf strokes, swaying should be avoided. A player who keeps his body still during the putting stroke, stands a better chance of becoming a good putter than one who lets it move back and forth with the action of the clubhead.

Stroke hard enough to reach the hole. You have heard the old adage, "never up, never in." Always play to sink the ball with the first putt. It is better to overrun than fall short. When direction is good the putt that has been hit too hard may hit the back of the cup and drop in. The putt played short requires another stroke.

Here are three suggestions that will aid the mediocre putter. Stand close to the ball, with a greater portion of the weight on the left foot. The duffer stands too far from the ball, losing control and direction. Don't grip too tightly. It stiffens the muscles and prevents relaxation. Swing the putter slowly and smoothly. Do not jab at the ball as if in a hurry to get the stroke over.

Keep the putter at right angles to the line.

Chip and Run-up Shots

THE CHIP SHOT is an exaggerated putt played with a more lofted club, such as a No. 3, 4, or 5 iron, or a club with even greater loft, as necessity arises.

The ball should be played far enough from the body so that the clubhead is not resting on its toe, yet close enough so that it is not resting on the heel. In other words, allow the clubhead to rest flush on the turf so that there will be no turning of the clubface in either direction as the ball is struck.

As in putting, take a comfortable position. Do not crouch over the ball or keep the feet far apart. An upright position, with the ball opposite the left heel, is much easier. Swing the clubhead low and close to the ground in the backstroke and the follow through. Swing more uprightly when a more lofted shot is necessary.

When playing the run-up shot, the ball should be played so that it will fall short of the putting surface and then roll to the hole. The ball is played back farther and the stroke is lightly downward. No pivot is required. The arms should be kept close to the sides, and only wrist and forearms used to make the swing. Of course, the length of the backswing varies according to the distance from the green.

The Left Heel

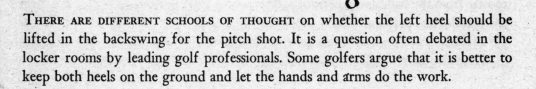

Do not consciously lift the left heel when playing a pitch shot.

THERE ARE DIFFERENT SCHOOLS OF THOUGHT on whether the left heel should be lifted in the backswing for the pitch shot. It is a question often debated in the locker rooms by leading golf professionals. Some golfers argue that it is better to keep both heels on the ground and let the hands and arms do the work.

A notable feature of Gene Sarazen's method of playing the pitch shot is that he uses little ankle and knee action, though he uses a free turn of the body from the hips up. He keeps the left heel on the ground.

Lifting of the left heel in the backswing should never be consciously done. It is the turning of the hips that causes the left knee to bend sufficiently to lift the left heel from the ground. Being mindful that the left heel must be lifted often causes the golfer to sway. Swaying must be avoided if the iron shot is to be a compact one.

In short approaches, where less hip action is required, the knee action at times is not enough to lift the heel from the ground. However, if the body-turn is sufficient to lift the heel, don't get the idea that you are executing the backswing for the pitch shot incorrectly. George Duncan, a great British golfer in his day, lifted the left heel, as did MacDonald Smith, one of the finest stylists the game has ever produced.

Impact

AT IMPACT, the position of the hands and arms should be similar to that at address.

Here the left arm should be firm, guiding the club through and maintaining the radius of the swing. The left hand has been in control of the swing up until now, but just before impact and thereafter, the right takes over, hitting against the left as the clubhead nears the ball. This snap of the wrists accelerates the speed of the clubhead, adding yardage to the drive.

The correct swing has the shoulders about parallel to the line of flight, with the right shoulder under the left.

Guard against getting the right side around too quickly, for body action will be wasted and the clubhead will be drawn across the ball. Also beware of putting your body action into the swing too late. The hips should be thrust forward, and the left leg straightened to brace the body as the arms swing the clubhead down against the ball. At this stage, both arms are straight, as the wrists and forearms do their part in speeding the clubhead through.

The left arm must not be allowed to collapse against the left side, for in a bent position, it cannot possibly swing the club out along the line of flight.

Shanking Avoided

Loosen the wrists when shanking creeps into the swing.

To MY MIND, the most disgusting and uncalled for shot in golf is that which is made by striking the ball with the neck or that part of the clubhead that bends into the shaft. It is commonly known as shanking or socketing.

Causes for this type of annoyance can be found in a hurried backswing, followed by a hurried downswing, which throws the hands and clubhead out beyond their correct paths.

Forcing the shot is another reason. This is because the golfer tries to make a number 5 iron do the work of a number 4. It will cause the golfer to be over-anxious to hit. This form of pressing can only result in a shanked shot.

Quitting on the shot, or attempting a stroke with no freedom of the wrists, is still another cause. Lack of wrist action will cause the clubhead to travel outside the line of flight. When wrists are locked, the golfer often attempts to make up lost power by a sway or lunge of the body toward the ball.

To avoid this demoralizing stroke, loosen up the wrists. Keep the hands close to the body. Some of the better golfers keep the hands so close that at times they brush their trouser legs.

The Head

Experts keep the eyes on spot where ball was teed long after impact.

THE HEAD is often referred to as the anchor of the golf swing. It keeps the club-head in its correct path.

You may argue that you have seen expert golfers move the head during the swing, and you are partially right. Fast action pictures have shown that good shot makers do move the head — but it is a slight movement, and it is a good idea to keep the head as close to the address position as possible all during the stroke. It is one way of acquiring a grooved swing.

Think of the head as the axle of a wheel, the club as a spoke, and the club-head as part of the rim. Any movement of the axle is transferred to the rim through the spoke. If the head, or axle, is lifted, control of the clubhead, or rim, is lost. Experts keep the head in the same position for some time after the ball is struck.

The head should not be held so rigidly that tension welds it to the top of the body. This is as bad a condition as moving the head during the swing. If the head is completely isolated from the rest of the body through rigidity, turning of the shoulders cannot take place in a proper swing.

When tension appears, and the head begins to pop up before the ball is struck, attempt to execute the stroke with more ease, starting the swing more slowly. Check the grip; tension might have started there.

The Hitting Region

Wrists stay cocked until hands have dropped below level of waist.

THE HITTING REGION is that part of the swing, just before impact, where the uncocking of the wrists takes place, adding speed to the clubhead. Through this part of the swing the clubhead travels at its maximum speed, faster and many times farther in relation to the hands.

Many golfers uncock their wrists too soon in the downswing, spending punch and power long before the club is in position to hit. When this takes places, one can be sure the right hand has assumed control at the start of the downswing.

The wrists should stay cocked until the hands have dropped below the waist and should not begin to unwind until the club is parallel to the ground.

At the start of the hitting region, the right arm has just started its straightening action, but the elbow is still bent and hugging the right side. It might be said that through the hitting region and not before is where the right hand comes into the stroke, whipping the clubhead through.

As already stated, if the wrists uncoil too soon, power is lost; if they are late in whipping the clubhead through, the clubface will hit the ball at an angle which will result in a pushed shot.

The Mental Side

How MANY TIMES have you started the season, or, after a long layoff from the game, resumed golfing by shooting a score that was better than expected? Shortly after, however, you find your score mounting. A good score early in the season can be attributed to the correct mental attitude. Your first "surprise" round probably was played completely relaxed and with the thought in mind that a score quite a few strokes above normal would be satisfactory.

Following this initial round, the golfer is bound to make a few bad shots. Then when he finds he is not quite sure of himself, he wonders what may have taken place to add a few bad ones to his score. His total mounts, and he begins to seek a cure for the trouble.

He takes inventory of his knowledge of the game and tries to remember all the "do's" and "don'ts" he has read and been told about. He reviews his swing. He contemplates his form. In desperation, he seeks the advice of his playing partner or pro, lamenting that he hasn't the faintest idea as to what he is doing wrong.

There is no player who can make a good golf stroke without giving a bit of thought to the action. So how can a player in such a state of mind think of the simplest fundamentals? With thoughts of that trap in front that must be carried crowding his mind, his head pops up long before the clubhead approaches the ball in the downswing. The result need not be mentioned. This player has listened to advice, but it has failed to penetrate a befuddled mind.

Let the player concentrate on but one thought in the swing — your pro or partner will tell you where you're off. If this is not the cure, select another suspected fault, concentrating on that point until the swing is working normally again.

Often golfers, in trying to cure one fault, exaggerate another. Suppose your body action is a bit faulty. You change the placement of your hands, forgetting the grip that stood you in good stead in the past. Now you have acquired another fault. In a desperate effort to affect a cure, you have added a third error.

Being mentally upset, the golfer has allowed tension to creep into the swing. To eliminate this tension, check and see that three points are relaxed. The wrists, the muscles controling the shoulders, and those in control of the lower part of the torso. If they are working freely, your shots will soon straighten out. By all means do not worry about a few badly-hit shots. Eliminate the thought of them from your mind, and concentrate on the shot at hand.

Balance

Settle well back on the heels at address.

AN IMPORTANT but often-neglected item in the golf swing is the matter of balance. Many golfers rise on their toes at the moment of impact. It is impossible to do this and maintain balance. Watch these golfers and you will note that they take a step forward with the right foot soon after the ball is struck. This is proof that they lacked balance throughout the swing, and that it was necessary to take this step to keep from falling over.

Only one heel should leave the ground at a time in the swing. Naturally it is the left in the backswing and the right in the downswing.

Do not reach for the ball, so that the weight will be pulled to the toes at address. It is better to settle well back on the heels where the golfer will find himself in a more comfortable position for the backstroke and the downswing. This also produces relaxation and banishes tension.

If you have the opportunity to watch star performers, you will see that the right heel is firm on the ground during the backswing, and the left is well anchored at the moment of impact.

Getting the Ball Into the Air

FAILURE TO GET THE BALL INTO THE AIR is a common fault of the beginner. It is hard to convince him that he should let the clubhead do the work. Often he keeps putting the ball closer and closer to the hole — playing it more off the left foot — at address, with the thought in mind that he has to boost the ball up in the air instead of allowing the loft on the face of the club to produce the desired elevation. He is surprised when advised to play the ball farther back — more off the right foot — and hit down on it.

Few golfers realize the important part backspin plays in getting the ball up. It is not only the loft of the clubhead that makes the ball climb — when the golfer depends only on the loft of the club to raise the ball, the trajectory will be considerably lower than if he hits down on it, imparting spin. Backspin sends the ball into the air because of the tendency of this spin to cause it to rise against air resistance, and the more loft to the club, the more backspin can be applied.

The swing should be more upright with less pivot. The clubhead is brought down more abruptly than when playing a wood, where the stroke should be a long sweep at the ball.

How Pros Correct Their Faults

DON'T GET THE IDEA that all golf professionals are perfect-game robots, and that they never make mistakes. Remember, to err is human, even with the pros. Some top-notch experts have natural faults which they must constantly guard against. A certain National Open Champion may have this fault corrected by now, but not so long ago he told me that all his life his leading fault was a closed face. He overcomes this error in his swing by placing the right hand more on top of the shaft, with the club well in the fingers, and accentuating the left hand pronation.

A Ryder Cupper says a fault he must watch out for is hooking. The way he corrects it is to see that, in making the backswing, his body turns with the club instead of picking the club up. And he keeps his feet anchored. He claims that

138

with this move working correctly, it gives him sufficient leverage to make the downswing without throwing the club from the top.

"This is the worst fault of the average golfer," he says. "They try to hit, instead of swing."

"You have to get the right position at the top of the backswing. If you do not arrive at this position, it makes the player swing very fast and throws the body and club out of time."

The average golfer making this move incorrectly has more or less a tendency to slice, but the good players, who use their hands well, naturally hook the ball.

A former National Open winner tells me the biggest trouble he has encountered over a period of time is the shortening of his backswing entirely too much. Being characteristically an abbreviated swinger, his backstroke became shorter and shorter, especially if he laid off competition for any length of time. As he shortened the backswing, the face of the club closed to such an extent that it caused hooking. He remedied this mistake by lengthening the backswing to a point where the club reached at least the horizontal position. A very good way of doing this, he says, is to watch for the clubhead out of the corner of the left eye. Of course, this should be done in practice until it becomes automatic and one loses the self-consciousness of the act.

Another Ryder Cupper, who has won his share of championships, says his faults are too numerous to mention, but thinks one of his basic faults in the longer shots is the failure to get a good pivot or a good wind-up of the body on the backswing. He says that a good wind-up, or coiling of the power muscles of the body, is essential to produce power and control with the greatest rhythm and timing and with the least strain on the player.

This expert has subconsciously feared losing his balance, and therefore has at times just maintained his position rather than have balance in motion. He most frequently shows this fault in an independent hand, arm, and shoulder swing away from the ball, instead of the more desirable start with the hips and legs. Starting too soon with the arms makes it difficult, if not impossible, to obtain the true wind-up as well as the proper co-ordination of the body, arms, and hands.

When experts run into trouble, they seek the advice of another professional. When you run into faults, do likewise.

DICTIONARY OF GOLF TERMS

To SAVE STROKES IN GOLF, the player should know all about the game and all of its equipment and peculiarities. For this reason, he should know the names of all pieces of equipment, the terms and phrases used to identify conditions, and the various words of golfdom, the free use of which identifies the golfer from the duffer. Hence, the following golf glossary:

Address – Position taken by a player in preparing to start a stroke.

Approach – A stroke played to the green.

Away – The ball farthest from the hole when more than one golfer is playing. Such a ball has priority of turn in playing unless ruled otherwise.

Bent – Grass primarily used on greens and teeing surfaces.

Birdie – Score for a hole played in one stroke under par.

Bogey – Used as an expression for a score of one over par on a hole.

Bogey Competition – A form of stroke competition in which golfers play against a fixed score at each hole of a stipulated round or rounds.

Brassie – A wooden club fitted with a metal sole used on the fairway. It has slightly more loft than the driver.

Bunker – A trap or hazard. That part of a depression where the soil is exposed and filled with sand.

Bye – Unplayed holes after a match has been won.

Casual Water – Temporary accumulation of water which is not recognized as a hazard on the course.

Cleek – A long-faced iron having little loft.

Dead – A ball is said to be dead when it lies so close to the hole that there is no doubt that it will be sunk with the next stroke.

Divot –Sod cut with clubhead after striking ball.

Dormie – A condition existing when a player or side is as many holes up as there are holes remaining to be played.

Eagle – A score for a hole two strokes under par.

Face – Striking surface of the clubhead.

Fairway – The well-kept portion of terrain between the tee and green, affording the player a favorable lie for the ball.

Fore – A warning to a player that a ball is about to be hit in his direction.

Foursome – A match in which two players play against two, each side playing one ball. This often is confused with a four-ball match, in which four players play.

Green – The putting surface, all ground except hazards within twenty yards of the hole being played as such.

Half Shot – A stroke in which the club is taken back to the vertical position as a maximum of swing.

Halved – When opponents hole out in the same number of strokes.

Hanging lie – A lie in which the ball is resting on a slope which slants toward the hole.

Hazard – Any bunker, water (except "causal water"), ditch, sand, or road obstruction between tee and green.

Head – Part of the club that strikes the ball, as distinguished from the shaft.

Heel – Part of the club at which shaft is fastened to the clubhead.

Hole – Round receptacle in green four and one-half inches in diameter and at least four inches deep. Often metal-lined. Units of play from tee to green. A round consists of eighteen holes or units.

Hole out – Putting the ball into the hole to finish the play for one unit.

Honor — The side or player having priority on a tee. Decided by lot or player or side winning previous hole.

Hook — To hit ball in a curve to the left of the intended line of flight.

Hosel — Hollow part of clubhead socket into which shaft is fitted.

Iron — A club which has a head of steel.

Lie — Manner in which a ball in play is resting. Also refers to angle of clubhead fastened to club.

Links — Term originally applied to a seaside golf course; now, any golf course.

Loft — Angle at which clubface is set from vertical. Used to lift ball into air in flight.

Loose impediment — Any obstruction not fixed or growing. Includes dung, worm casts, mole hills, snow, and ice.

Marker — A scorer, not a referee. Also an object determining forward limits of teeing ground.

Mashie — Usual number 5 iron, loft set at about 40 degrees.

Match — Contest between two or more players or sides.

Match Play — Competition in which results are determined by the number of holes won.

Medal Play — Stroke competition in which results are determined by number of strokes played.

Nassau — A system of scoring: one point allotted for first nine; one point for second nine, and one point for the 18 holes.

Neck — Part of club where shaft joins the head.

Niblick — A heavy, wide iron club with ample degree of loft.

Odd — Indicates a term for the player who has already played one stroke more than his opponent.

Out of Bounds — Ground on which play is prohibited.

Par — Standard score for a hole.

Penalty Stroke — A stroke added to score of a side under certain rules.

Provisional Ball — A ball played after previous ball probably has been lost or is unplayable.

Pull — To hit the ball straight, but to the left of the line.

Push — To hit the ball straight, but to the right of the line. This differs from the slice; a pushed shot is hit straight to the right, and doesn't curve.

Putt — Playing a stroke on the green.

Putter — Club designed for putting. Lie is upright with very little loft.

Rough — Heavy long grass fringing green or fairway, where little effort has been made to condition it for play.

Rub of Green — An expression for a condition arising when a ball in motion is stopped or deflected by an agency outside the match.

Sclaff — To scrape or cut turf with clubhead before impact with ball.

Shaft — Handle of the club.

Shank — To hit the ball with the socket or neck of the club.

Slice — A clockwise spin which causes ball to curve to the right of the intended line.

Sole — Bottom of the clubhead. Act of placing the club on the ground at address.

Spoon — One of the wooden clubs having a thin head, shallow face, and considerable loft.

Square — A match that is even; reference to a stance in which both feet are in a line parallel to the line of flight.

Stance — Position of the feet in stroking.

Stroke — Forward movement of the club made with the intention of striking the ball.

Stroke Play — Same as medal play.

Stymie — When, on the putting green, the opponent's ball lies in line of a player's putt to the hole, providing that ball is not within six inches of the other, and the nearer ball not within six inches of the hole.

Swing — Action by a player in stroking the ball.

Tee — Wooden peg used in starting play from teeing surface.

Teeing Ground — Often called the tee. Starting place for the hole to be played. Indicated in front by two markers. A rectangular space of the depth of two club-lengths directly behind the line indicated by the markers.

Threesome — A match in which two players play alternate strokes with one ball opposing a single player. Often confused with a threeball match in which three players play, each playing a ball.

Toe — Forward part of clubhead.

Top — To strike ball above center.

Twosome — Popularly used to describe a "single," (see Definition 1, page 146) in which one player plays against another.

Whiff — Missing the ball entirely.

Waggle — Preliminary action of flexing the wrists, causing the club to swing forward and backward.

(1) No one should move or talk or stand close to or directly behind the ball or the hole when a player is making a stroke.

(2) The player who has the honour should be allowed to play before his opponent tees his ball.

(3) No player should play until the party in front are out of range.

(4) When the result of a hole has been determined players should immediately leave the putting green.

(5) Players while looking for a lost ball should allow other matches coming up to pass them; they should signal to the players following them to pass, and having given such a signal, they should not continue their play until these players have passed and are out of range.

(6) A player should see that any turf cut or displaced by him is at once replaced and pressed down.

(7) Players should carefully fill up all holes made in a bunker.

(8) Players should see that their caddies do not injure the holes by standing close to them when the ground is soft or in replacing the flagstick.

(9) A player who has incurred a penalty should intimate the fact to his opponent as soon as possible.

(10) Players should at all times play without undue delay.

A competitor who by delay in play unfairly interferes with the play of any other competitor shall be disqualified, in either match play or stroke play. U.S.G.A.

Players who do not continue in the match play rounds of a tournament should be considered to have forfeited any prize they may have won in the qualifying round. U.S.G.A.

RULES OF THE GAME OF GOLF

AS APPROVED BY

THE UNITED STATES GOLF ASSOCIATION

AND BY THE

ROYAL AND ANCIENT GOLF CLUB

OF ST. ANDREWS

* Except that part of the preamble and note on page 146 known as the fourteen-club rule, and the amendment to Rule 31 and footnotes thereto.

RULES OF THE GAME OF GOLF

The game of golf consists in a ball being played from the teeing ground into the hole by successive strokes, with clubs (not exceeding fourteen in number) and balls made in conformity with the directions laid down in the clause on "Form and Make of Golf Clubs and Balls." U.S.G.A.

Penalty for violation in match play and stroke play— Disqualification. U.S.G.A.

DEFINITIONS

Side

(1) A "side" consists of one or more players.

NOTE—*In Rules 1 to 35 the term "side" refers to one or more players playing one ball, as in a threesome or a foursome. In the Rules for Best Ball and Four-Ball Matches the term "side" refers to two or more players each playing a ball against an opponent or opponents. U.S.G.A.*

If one player play against another, the match is called "a single."

If one play against two, each side playing one ball, the match is called "a threesome."

If two play against two, each side playing one ball, the match is called "a foursome."

If three play against one another, each playing his own ball, the match is called "a three-ball match."

If one plays against the better or best ball of two or more players, the match is called "a best ball match."

If two play their better ball against the better ball of two other players, the match is called "a four-ball match."

Advice

(2) "Advice" is any counsel or suggestion which could influence a player in determining his play, the choice of a club, or the method of making a stroke.

Information as to the Rules of Golf or information indicating the line to the hole is not considered advice.

Course

(3) The "course" is the whole area within which play is permitted; more particularly, it is the ground between the holes which is specially prepared for play.

Teeing Ground

(4) The "teeing ground" is the starting place for the hole to be played. The front shall be indicated by two marks, and the teeing ground is a rectangular space of the depth of two club-lengths directly behind the line indicated by the two marks.

Through the Green

(5) "Through the green" is the whole of the course except the teeing ground (Definition 4), the putting green (Definition 10) and hazards (Definition 6).

Hazard

(6) A "hazard" is any bunker, water (except "casual water"), ditch, sand or road. Sand blown on to the grass, or sprinkled on the course for its preservation, bare patches, scrapes, tracks and paths, snow, ice and casual water are not hazards.

A "bunker" is that part of a depression in the ground where the soil is exposed, and sometimes covered with sand. Grass in a bunker is not part of the hazard, unless so defined by local rule.

It is the duty of the authorities in charge of a course accurately to define the extent of the hazards.

The word "tracks" as used in Definition 6 means marks left by the occasional passage of vehicles or of greenkeepers' equipment, as distinguished from a roadway constructed or established by usage and customarily used for passage from and to definite points.

Casual Water

(7) "Casual water" is any temporary accumulation of water which is not one of the ordinary and recognized hazards of the course.

The definition of "water" in the term "casual water" is any water which interferes with the lie of the ball or the stance of the player. R. & A.

Out of Bounds

(8) "Out of bounds" is ground on which play is prohibited, but it does not include ground under repair.

Ball, When Out of Bounds

(9) A ball is "out of bounds" when the greater part of it lies outside the course.

Putting Green

(10) The "putting green" is all ground, excepts hazards, within twenty yards of the hole being played.

Hole

(11) The hole shall be 4¼ inches in diameter and at least 4 inches deep. If a metal lining be used, it shall be sunk below the lip of the hole, and its outer diameter shall not exceed 4¼ inches.

Linings (cups) shall be sunk approximately one inch below the putting green surface unless the nature of the soil makes it impractical to so do, in which case the minimum depth shall be approximately three-quarters of an inch. Linings must be of metal, but may be of any color. Cardboard, composition or other linings than metal may not be used. U.S.G.A.

Loose Impediments

(12) The term "loose impediments" denotes any obstructions not fixed or growing, and includes dung, worm-casts, mole-hills, snow and ice.

Loose stones are "loose impediments." R. & A.
Rocks embedded in the ground come under the head of "things fixed." Rule 15. R. & A.
A worm is a "loose impediment" and may be lifted. R. & A.

Stroke

(13) A "stroke" is the forward movement of the club made with the intention of striking the ball.

Penalty Stroke

(14) A "penalty stroke" is a stroke added to the score of a side under certain rules, and does not affect the rotation of play.

Honour

(15) The side which plays first from a teeing ground is said to have the "honour."

Teeing

(16) In "teeing," the ball may be placed on the ground, or on sand or other substance in order to raise it off the ground.

Addressing the Ball

(17) A player has "addressed the ball" when he has taken his stance by placing his feet on the ground in position for and preparatory to striking at the ball, and has grounded his club, or, if in a hazard, when he has taken his stance preparatory to striking at the ball.

In Play

(18) A ball is "in play" as soon as the player has made a stroke on the teeing ground, and it remains in play until holed out, except when it is out of bounds, lost, or lifted in accordance with the rules.

A player must hole out with the ball driven from the tee unless it be lost or played out of bounds or into a water hazard or casual water or become unfit for play. In any such case a player may substitute another ball. A ball lifted from a water hazard or casual water or from ground under repair may be cleaned; otherwise a player may not clean a ball except to the extent necessary for identification.

Ball Deemed to Move

(19) A ball is deemed to have moved if it leave its position and come to rest in any other place.

Ball Lost

(20) A ball is "lost" if it be not found within five minutes after the player's side or his or their caddies have begun to search for it, and if subsequently found may not be played.

Terms Used in Reckoning

(21) The reckoning of strokes is kept by the terms — "the odd," "two more," "three more," etc., and "one off three," "one off two," "the like." The reckoning of holes is kept by the terms — so many "holes up," or "all even" and so many "to play."

A side is said to be "dormie" when it is as many holes up as there are holes remaining to be played.

Committee, Referee, Marker

(22) The "committee" is the committee in charge of the competition.

A "referee" is a person who has been authorised by the committee or agreed upon by the players to accompany a match to decide questions of golfing law. Whether an appeal be made or not a referee shall take cognisance of any breach of rule that he may observe or which may be reported to him by any person or persons appointed by himself to assist him. A referee shall also decide questions of fact after consultation (if necessary) with anyone so appointed.

A "marker" is a scorer and is not a referee.

A referee or a marker shall never attend the flagstick, stand at or mark the hole. U.S.G.A.

Rub of the Green

(23) A "rub of the green" occurs when a ball in motion is stopped or deflected by any agency outside the match.

RULE 1

Conditions

In match play the game is played by holes:

Except as otherwise provided for in the rules, a hole is won by the side which holes its ball in fewer strokes than the opposing side, and a hole is halved if both sides hole out in the same number of strokes.

A match consists of a round of eighteen holes (unless otherwise decreed) and is won by the side which is leading by a number of holes greater than the number of holes remaining to be played, and is halved if each side win the same number of holes.

In competitions players shall not agree to exclude the operation of any rule or local rule, nor to waive any penalty incurred.

Penalty—Disqualification of both sides.

In competitions players using clubs or balls which are not in conformity with the clause on "Form and Make of Golf Clubs and Balls" shall be disqualified.

NOTES: *Practice Stroke—A practice stroke with a ball during a round is not permissible, nor is rolling a ball by hand or other similar act to test a putting surface; however, a player may try a putt after he and his companions hole out provided play is not delayed. Penalty, in match play and stroke play—Disqualification. U.S.G.A.*

Practice Swing—A practice swing (without a ball) may be taken any place on the course provided the player does not violate the provisions of Rules 10, 15, 21(1), and 25. U.S.G.A.

Priority on the Course

In the absence of special by-laws for the regulation of play, matches constituted of singles, threesomes, or foursomes shall have precedence of and be entitled to pass any other kind of match. A single player has no standing, and shall always give way to a match of any kind.

Any match playing a whole round shall be entitled to pass a match playing a shorter round.

If a match fail to keep its place on the course, and lose in distance more than one clear hole on the players in front, it shall allow the match following to pass, on request being made.

TEEING GROUND

RULE 2

The Honour

(1) A match begins by each side playing a ball from the first teeing ground in the order of the draw. In the absence of a draw the option of taking the honour shall, if necessary, be decided by lot.

The side which wins a hole shall take the honour at the next teeing ground. If a hole has been halved the side which had the honour at the previous teeing ground shall retain it.

When a match has been won, the winner shall take the honour at the next teeing ground.

In any handicap match the honour is determined by the net scores of the preceding hole. U.S.G.A.

Opponent May Recall Ball

(2) If a player play when his opponent should have had the honour, or play a ball from outside the limits of the teeing ground, the ball may be at once recalled by the opposing side and may be re-teed without penalty.

For stroke play see Stroke Rule 7.

Stance

(3) A player may take his stance outside the limits of the teeing ground to play a ball within these limits.

Ball Falling off Tee

(4) If a ball, when not in play, fall off a tee, or be knocked off a tee by the player in addressing it, it may be re-teed without penalty; if the ball be struck under these circumstances, whether moving or not, the stroke shall be counted but no penalty shall be incurred.

RULE 3

Order of Play in Threesome and Foursome

In a threesome or foursome the partners shall strike off alternately from the teeing grounds, and thereafter the players shall strike alternately during the play of each hole.

Penalty in match play—Loss of hole.
Penalty in stroke play—Disqualification.
A penalty stroke does not affect the rotation of play.
(See Definition 14.)

RULE 4

Advice

(1) A player may not ask for nor take any action which may result in his receiving advice (Definition 2) except from his caddie, his partner, or his partner's caddie.

Penalty in match play—Loss of hole.
Penalty in stroke play—Disqualification. (Stroke Rule 6.)

Information as to Strokes Played

(2) A player is entitled at any time during the play of a hole to ascertain from his opponent the number of strokes the latter has played; if the opponent give wrong information as to the number of strokes he has played, he shall lose the hole, unless he correct his mistake before the player has played his next stroke.

See Rule 33.

Forecaddie

(3) A player may employ a forecaddie, but may not receive advice (Definition 2) from him.

Penalty in match play—Loss of hole.
Penalty in stroke play—Disqualification.

Indicating Line of Play

(4) A player may at any time have the line to the hole indicated to him, but no mark shall be placed nor shall anyone stand on the proposed line, in order to indicate it, while the stroke is being made. The flagstick may at any time be held up so as to indicate the position of the hole.

Penalty in match play—Loss of hole.
Penalty in stroke play—Two strokes.

RULE 5

Ball to be Fairly Struck at

The ball must be fairly struck at with the head of the club and must not be pushed, scraped or spooned.

Penalty in match play—Loss of hole.
Penalty in stroke play—Two strokes.

RULE 6

Ball Played Wherever it Lies

A ball must be played wherever it lies or the hole be given up, except as otherwise provided for in the rules or local rules.

NOTE. — For a lost or unplayable ball see Rule 22; for a ball out of bounds see Rule 23.

RULE 7

The Ball Farther from the Hole Played First

When the balls are in play, the ball farther from the hole shall be played first. Through the green or in a hazard if a player play when his opponent should have played, the opponent may at once recall the stroke, and a ball shall be dropped without penalty as near as possible to the place from which the previous stroke was played.

When the balls are equi-distant from the hole the option of playing shall be decided by lot.

For teeing ground see Rule 2.

For putting green see Rule 31.

RULE 8

Dropping and Placing

When a ball through the green is lifted and dropped under the rules, it must be dropped as near as possible to the place where it lay and must come to rest not nearer to the hole.

If the ball when dropped come to rest nearer to the hole it shall be re-dropped without penalty, and in cases where it is impossible owing to the configuration of the ground to prevent a dropped ball from rolling nearer to the hole the ball shall be placed.

A ball lifted from the putting green must be replaced on the spot from which it was lifted, except as otherwise provided for in the rules.

For hazards see Rule 25.
Penalty in match play—Loss of hole.
Penalty in stroke play—Two strokes.

How to Drop a Ball

A ball shall be dropped in the following manner: — The player himself shall drop it. He shall face the hole, stand erect, and drop the ball behind him over his shoulder.
Penalty in match play—Loss of hole.
Penalty in stroke play—Two strokes.

If, in the act of dropping, the ball touch the player, he shall incur no penalty, and, if it roll into a hazard, the player may re-drop the ball without penalty.

RULE 9

Ball Not to be Touched Except as Provided for in Rules

(1) A ball in play may not be touched before the hole is played out, except as provided for in the rules.
See Definition 18 and note.
Compare Rule 12 (3).
Penalty in match play—Loss of hole.
Penalty in stroke play—Two strokes.

Ball Not to be Touched Except in Addressing

The player may, without penalty, touch his ball with his club in the act of addressing it, provided he does not move the ball.

Ball Not to be Touched Except for Identification

A ball in play may, after intimation is given to the opponent, be lifted for the purpose of identification, but it must be replaced on the spot from which it was lifted.
For stroke play—See Stroke Rule 12.

Opponent's Ball Moved by Player's Ball

(2) If the player's ball move the opponent's ball, the opponent, if he choose, may drop, or in a hazard or on the putting green may place a ball as near as possible to the spot from which the original ball was moved, without penalty, but this must be done before another stroke is played by either side.

RULE 10

Removal of Irregularities of Surface

Irregularities of surface which could in any way affect the player's stroke shall not be removed nor pressed down by the player, his partner, or either of their caddies; a player is, however, always entitled to place his feet firmly on the ground when taking his stance, but he is not allowed to build a stance.
Penalty in match play—Loss of hole.
Penalty in stroke play—Two strokes.

RULE 11

Removal of Obstructions

Any flagstick, guidepost, implement, vehicle, bridge, bridge planking, seat, hut, shelter or similar obstruction may be removed. A ball moved in removing such an obstruction shall be lifted and dealt with as provided for in Rule 8 without penalty.

A ball lying on or touching such an obstruction, or lying on or touching clothes, or ground under repair, or a drain cover, hydrant, hydrant cover, or exposed water pipe, or lying in a hole made by the greenkeeper, may be lifted and dealt with as provided for in Rule 8 without penalty.

If the player's stroke be interfered with by any such obstruction which is immovable and which is within two club-lengths of his ball, the ball may be lifted and dropped, or on the putting green placed, not more than two club-lengths from the obstacle, but not nearer to the hole, without penalty.

For hazards see Rule 25.
The following are obstructions under Rule 11:—material piled for removal, including a pile of cut grass; guy wires and other material used to support trees and poles

and other objects; artificial poles for electricity, telephone, telegraph, etc.; artificial steps not made entirely of earth (but not steps of buildings which are not classified as obstructions under Rule 11); parts of bridges and abutments not in confines of hazards; protective screens, ropes, stakes and railings, and stakes defining hazards and boundaries (but not fences or fence posts); parts of water systems and their covers, containers, bases and supports, including fountains, pumps, pump-houses, tanks, valves, sprinklers, drains, hoses; traps for insects and animals; benches; tee boxes and ball-washers; boards for scores and notices; tents; refreshment stands; paper, bottles and similar artificial objects. U.S.G.A.

If a ball cannot be found in ground under repair, it must be considered a lost ball under Rule 22. U.S.G.A.

RULE 12

Removal of Loose Impediments

(1) Except when the ball lies in or touches a hazard any loose impediment may be removed without penalty.

(2) If the ball move after any loose impediment lying within a club-length of the ball through the green has been touched by the player, his partner, or either of their caddies, the player shall be deemed to have caused the ball to move and the penalty shall be one stroke.

For hazards see Rule 25.

For putting green see Rule 28.

Ball Accidentally Moved

(3) When a ball is in play, if a player, or his partner, or either of their caddies accidentally move it, or by touching anything cause it to move, the penalty shall be one stroke.

Ball Moving after Club Grounded

(4) If a ball in play move after the player has addressed it he shall be deemed to have caused it to move, and the penalty shall be one stroke.

NOTE. — If the player has lifted a loose impediment [see Rules 12 (1) and 28 (1)] and the ball has not moved until the player has addressed it, he shall only be deemed to have caused the ball to move under Section (4) of this Rule, and the penalty shall be one stroke.

RULE 13

Playing a Moving Ball

A player shall not play while his ball is moving, except in the case of a teed ball (Rule 2), or a ball struck twice (Rule 14), or a ball in water (Rule 26). When the ball only begins to move while the player is making his backward or forward swing, he shall incur no penalty under this Rule, but he is not exempted from the provisions of Rule 12 or Rule 28 (1).

Penalty in match play—Loss of hole.
Penalty in stroke play—Two strokes.

RULE 14

Striking Ball Twice

If a player when making a stroke, hit the ball twice, he shall count the stroke and a penalty stroke in addition.

RULE 15

Moving or Bending Fixed or Growing Objects

Before striking at a ball in play, a player shall not improve the position of his ball by moving, bending, or breaking anything fixed or growing, except (1) so far as is necessary to enable him fairly to take his stance in addressing the ball, and (2) in making his backward or forward swing. The club may only be grounded lightly, and not pressed on the ground.

Penalty in match play—Loss of hole.
Penalty in stroke play—Two strokes.
For practice strokes and swings, see Notes to Rule 1.
In grounding a club, a player may only ground his club lightly. Drawing it back and forward across the line of play is illegal and entails a penalty of the loss of the hole in match play and a penalty of two strokes in stroke competition. U.S.G.A.
Undue pressure in grounding a club entails a like penalty. R. & A.

RULE 16

Balls within a Club-Length of Each Other

When a ball not on the putting green lies within a club-length of another ball, the ball lying nearer to the hole may, at the option of either the player or the opponent, be lifted until the other ball is played, and shall then be replaced as near as possible to the place where it lay.

If either ball be accidentally moved in complying with this Rule, no penalty shall be incurred, and the ball so moved shall be replaced.

If the lie of the lifted ball be altered in playing the other ball, the lifted ball may be placed as near as possible to the place where it lay and in a lie similar to that which it originally occupied.

RULE 17

Moving Ball Stopped

(1) In the event of a rub of the green (Definition 23) the ball shall be played from where it lies.

Ball Lodging in Anything Moving

(2) If a ball lodge in *anything moving*, a ball shall be dropped, or if on the putting green, placed, as near as possible to the spot where the object was when the ball lodged in it, without penalty.

Ball at Rest Displaced by Outside Agency

(3) If the lie of a ball *at rest* be altered by any agency outside the match except wind, the player shall drop a ball as near as possible to the place where it lay, without penalty; and if the ball be displaced on the putting green, it shall be replaced without penalty.

This section applies to a ball that has been stepped on and driven into the ground by a spectator. U.S.G.A.

RULE 18

Ball Interfered with by Opponent, etc.

If a player's ball strike or be moved by an opponent or his caddie, or his clubs, the opponent's side shall lose the hole, except as provided for in Rules 9 (2), 16, 21 (3), 31 (1), 32 (2), and 33.

RULE 19

Ball Striking the Player, etc.

If a player's ball strike himself, or his partner, or either of their caddies, or forecaddies, or their clubs, his side shall lose the hole.

Penalty in stroke play—Two strokes. (Stroke Rule 9.)

RULE 20

Playing Opponent's Ball

(1) If a player play the opponent's ball his side shall lose the hole, unless: —

(*a*) the opponent then play the player's ball, in which case the penalty is cancelled, and the hole shall be played out with the balls thus exchanged.

(*b*) the mistake occur through wrong information given by an opponent or his caddie, in which case there shall be no penalty; if the mistake be discovered before the opponent has played his next stroke, it shall be rectified by dropping, or on the putting green, placing a ball as near as possible to the place where the opponent's ball lay.

Playing Ball outside the Match

(2) If a player play a stroke with the ball of anyone not engaged in the match, and the mistake be discovered and intimated to his opponent before his opponent has played his next stroke, there shall be no penalty; if the mistake be not discovered and so intimated until after the opponent has played his next stroke, the player's side shall lose the hole.

For stroke play—See Stroke Rule 8.
For practice strokes and swings, see Notes to Rule 1. U.S.G.A. recommends that each competitor place an identification mark upon his ball.

RULE 21

Looking for Ball in Bent, etc.

(1) If a ball lie in fog, bent, bushes, long grass, or the like, only so much thereof shall be touched as will enable the player to find his ball.

A player is entitled to find his ball. Once found he is not of necessity entitled to a sight of the ball when playing his stroke but must play the ball as it lies. U.S.G.A.

In Sand

(2) If a ball be completely covered by sand, only so much thereof may be removed as will enable the player to see the top of the ball; if the ball be touched in removing the sand, no penalty shall be incurred.

Accidentally Moved by Opponent in Search

(3) If a player or his caddie when searching for an opponent's ball accidentally touch or move it, no penalty shall be incurred, and the ball, if moved, shall be replaced.

RULE 22

Lost and Unplayable Ball

(1) Except as provided for in Rule 27, if a ball be lost or be deemed by the player to be unplayable, the player shall play his next stroke as nearly as possible at the spot from which the ball which is lost or unplayable was played, adding a penalty stroke to the score for the hole.

If the stroke was played from the teeing ground, a ball may be teed; if from through the green or a hazard it shall be dropped, and if on the putting green it shall be placed.

Provisional Ball Played

(2) If a ball has been played on to a part of the course where it is likely to be lost or unplayable, the player may, in order to save delay, at once play another ball provisionally in the manner provided for in this Rule, but if the first ball be neither lost nor deemed unplayable it shall continue in play without penalty.

The player may continue to play with a provisional ball until he reaches the place where the previous ball is likely to be.

NOTE. — A provisional ball may only be played under the second section of this Rule before the player or his partner goes forward to search for the ball which has been played with the previous stroke.

Penalty for breach of this Rule in match play—Loss of hole.
In stroke play, penalty for breach of this Rule, as to lost ball—disqualification. For procedure as to an unplayable ball and penalty in stroke play, see Stroke Rule 11.
A person outside the match may point out the location of the ball for which search is being made.
NOTE — ORDER OF PLAY. — Whenever a player having the honour has played a stroke (see Definition 13) from the teeing ground—no matter what the result may be—the opponent must play the next stroke. The playing of a provisional ball does not in any way affect the order in which the sides play, and if a player plays a provisional ball before his opponent has played a stroke the opponent may at once recall the stroke. U.S.G.A.

There is no limitation as to the number of strokes the player may play with a provisional ball before arriving at the approximate location of the ball believed to be lost or unplayable. U.S.G.A.

The player is the sole judge as to when his ball is unplayable. It may be declared unplayable at any place on the course except in a water hazard or in casual water. U.S.G.A.

RULE 23

Ball Out of Bounds

(1) If a ball lie out of bounds the player shall play his next stroke as nearly as possible at the spot from which the ball which is out of bounds was played, adding a penalty stroke to the score for the hole.

If the stroke was played from the teeing ground a ball may be teed; in all other cases a ball shall be dropped.

In the case of a ball played out of bounds, the penalty stroke may be remitted by local rule (see note).

See Definitions 8 and 9.

Provisional Ball Played

(2) If a player, after making a stroke, consider that his ball may be out of bounds, he may, in order to save delay, at once play another ball provisionally in the manner provided for in this Rule, but if it be discovered that his first ball is not out of bounds, it shall continue in play without penalty, provided the ball is not deemed unplayable.

NOTE. – *Out of Bounds.* – If the penalty stroke has been remitted by a local rule and a provisional ball has been played under these conditions, on reaching the place where the first ball is likely to be, if the player or his opponent be still in doubt, the player is not entitled to presume that the first ball is out of bounds till he has made a search of five minutes.

A provisional ball may only be played under the second section of this Rule before the player or his partner goes forward to search for the ball which has been played with the previous stroke.

The player may continue to play with a provisional ball until he reaches the place where the previous ball is likely to be.

NOTE — ORDER OF PLAY. — Whenever a player having the honour has played a stroke (see Definition 13) from the teeing ground—no matter what the result may be—the opponent must play the next stroke. The playing of a provisional ball does not in any way affect the order in which the sides play, and if a player plays a provisional ball before his opponent has played a stroke the opponent may at once recall the stroke. U.S.G.A.

Ascertaining Location of Ball

(3) A player has the right at any time of ascertaining whether his opponent's ball is out of bounds or not.

Standing Out of Bounds

(4) A player may stand out of bounds to play a ball lying within bounds.

Penalty for violation of Rule 23 in match play is loss of hole and in stroke play is disqualification. U.S.G.A.

RULE 24

Ball Unfit for Play

If a ball be so damaged as to be unfit for play, the player may change it on intimating to his opponent his intention to do so. Mud adhering to a ball shall not be considered as making it unfit for play.

For stroke play see Stroke Rule 12.

Whether or not a ball be unfit for play is a question of fact, and must be decided by the referee. If there be no referee a dispute if arising in match play must be decided as provided in Rule 35, and if arising in stroke play as provided in Stroke Rules 5 (3) and 16. U.S.G.A.

Cleaning a ball when in play entails a penalty of two strokes in stroke competition and the loss of the hole in match play, except under special rulings by committee in charge. U.S.G.A.

See Definition 18 and note.

HAZARDS

RULE 25

Hazards

When a ball lies in or touches a hazard the club shall not touch the ground, nor shall anything be touched or moved, before the player strikes at the ball, subject to the following exceptions: —

(1) The player may place his feet firmly on the ground for the purpose of taking his stance.

(2) In addressing the ball, or in the backward or forward swing, any grass, bent, bush, tree or other growing substance, or the side of a bunker, wall, paling, or other immovable obstacle may be touched.

(3) Steps or blanks placed in a hazard by the green committee for access to or egress from such hazard, or any obstruction mentioned in Rule 11, may be removed, and if a ball be moved in so doing, it shall be replaced without penalty.

If any fixed steps or plank interfere with a player's stroke the ball may be lifted and placed as near as possible to the spot where it lay in a similar lie and position without penalty.

See note to Rule 11.

(4) Any loose impediment not in or touching the hazard may be lifted.

(5) The player shall be entitled to find his ball as provided for by Rule 21.

Penalty in match play—Loss of hole.
Penalty in stroke play—Two strokes.
See Rule 16.

There is no penalty for the player smoothing irregularities in the hazard made by his footprints or the soil displaced by his stroke, provided nothing is done that improves the lie of the ball or assists the player in his subsequent play of the hole. U.S.G.A.

A recognized water hazard cannot be "out of bounds." R. & A.

WATER

RULE 26

Ball Moving in Water

When a ball is in water a player may, without penalty, strike at it while it is moving, but he must not delay to make his stroke in order to allow the wind or current to better the position of the ball.

Penalty in match play—Loss of hole.
Penalty in stroke play—Two strokes.

RULE 27

Ball in Water Hazard or in Casual Water in a Hazard

(1) If a ball lie or be lost in a recognised water hazard (whether the ball lie in water or not) or in casual water in a hazard, the player may drop a ball, under penalty of one stroke either (*a*) behind the hazard, keeping the spot at which the ball crossed the margin of the hazard between himself and the hole, or (*b*) in the hazard, keeping the spot at which the ball entered the water between himself and the hole. If the ball was played from the teeing ground a ball may be teed, under penalty of one stroke, as nearly as possible at the spot from which the original ball was played.

Ice on the putting green or through the green is considered "casual water." R. & A.

NOTE — WATER HAZARD. — A ball that has lodged in a water hazard may not be treated in accordance with Rule 22. Rule 27 is a specific rule covering the conditions under which a ball in the water hazard must be played. A provisional ball may not be played under Rule 27. If a player decides to drop or tee a ball and play it, he must continue with this ball and is not allowed the privilege of playing his original ball if found to be playable in the hazard. U.S.G.A.

There is no limitation as to how far behind a hazard a ball may be dropped. U.S.G.A.

Grass within the boundaries of a water hazard is part of the hazard and when a ball lies thereon the club shall not touch the ground, etc. Rule 25. It is the duty of local committees to indicate the boundaries of water hazards by white stakes or otherwise. U.S.G.A.

Ball in Casual Water Through the Green

(2) If a ball lie or be lost in casual water through the green, the player may drop a ball, without penalty, on dry ground as near as possible to the spot where the ball lay, but not nearer to the hole.

If a ball when dropped roll into the water, it may be re-dropped without penalty.

Ball in Casual Water on the Putting Green

(3) If a ball on the putting green lie in casual water, or if casual water intervene between a ball lying on the putting green and the hole, the ball may be played where it lies, or it may be lifted without penalty and placed in the nearest position to where it lay which is not nearer to the hole and which affords a stroke to the hole without casual water intervening.

Water Interfering with Stance

(4) A ball lying so near to casual water that the water interferes with the player's stance may be treated as if it lay in the casual water, under the preceding sections of this Rule.

Want of Space to Drop

(5) If it be impossible from want of space in which to play, or from any other cause, for a player to drop a ball in conformity with sections (1) and (2) of this Rule, or to place it in conformity with section (3), he shall "drop" or "place" as nearly as possible within the limits laid down in these sections, but not nearer to the hole.

Penalty for breach of Rule—Loss of hole.
Penalty for breach of Rule in stroke play—Two strokes.

PUTTING GREEN

RULE 28

Removal of Loose Impediments

(1) If the player's ball, when on the putting green, move after any loose impediment lying within six inches of it has been touched by the player, his partner, or either of their caddies, he player shall be deemed to have caused it to move and the penalty shall be one stroke.

(2) In moving any loose impediment with the club it must not be laid with more than its own weight upon the ground, nor must anything be pressed down either with the club or in any other way.

Touching Line of Putt

(3) The line of the putt must not be touched, except by placing the club immediately in front of the ball in the act of addressing it, and as above authorised.

Penalty in match play—Loss of hole.
Penalty in stroke play— Two strokes.
It is not permissible to touch the ground behind the hole in order to point out the line of a putt. R. & A.

RULE 29

Direction for Putting

(1) When the player's ball is on the putting green, the player's caddie, his partner or his partner's caddie may, before the stroke is played, point out a direction for putting, but in doing this they shall not touch the ground on the proposed line of the stroke. No mark shall be placed anywhere on the putting green.

Testing the surface especially prepared for putting by roughing or scraping it with a club or otherwise will be considered as placing a mark on the putting green, and the player will be subject to the penalties of this Rule. U.S.G.A.

For practice strokes and swings, see Notes to Rule 1.

Shielding Ball from Wind

(2) Any player or caddie engaged in the match may stand at the hole, but no player or caddie shall endeavor by moving or otherwise to influence the action of the wind upon the ball.

A player is, however, always entitled to send his own caddie to stand at the hole while he plays his stroke.

Penalty in match play—Loss of hole.
Penalty in stroke play—Two strokes.

RULE 30

Opponent's Ball to be at Rest

When the player's ball lies on the putting green, he shall not play until the opponent's ball is at rest.

Penalty in match play—Loss of hole.
Penalty in stroke play—Two strokes.

RULE 31

Ball within Six Inches of Hole or Other Ball

(1) *When the balls are on the putting green and the nearer ball lies within six inches of the hole, or one ball lies within six inches of the other (the distance in both cases to be measured from the nearest points),* the ball lying nearer to the hole may, at the option of either the player or the opponent, be lifted until the other ball is played, and the lifted ball shall then be replaced as near as possible to the place where it lay. If either ball be accidentally moved in complying with this Rule, no penalty shall be incurred and the ball so moved shall be replaced.

Note (1)—That part of the above subdivision (1) in Italics is substituted permanently by the U.S.G.A. in place of the following language: "When the balls lie within six inches of each other on the putting green (the distance to be measured from their nearest points)." The above substitution has not, however, been adopted by the R. & A.

Note (2)—A player is laid a stymie if, on the putting green, the opponent's ball lies in the line of his putt to the hole, provided the balls be not within six inches of each other and the nearer ball be not within six inches of the hole. U.S.G.A.

Playing Out of Turn

(2) On the putting green, if a player play when his opponent should have played, the stroke shall be at once recalled by the opponent and the ball replaced.

NOTE.—For a ball which is displaced on a putting green, see Rule 17 (2) and (3).

For a player playing the opponent's ball on the putting green see Rule 20 (1).

Casual Water

For casual water on the putting green, see Rule 27 (3).

RULE 32

Removal of Flagstick

(1) Either side is entitled to have the flagstick removed at any time, but a player may always have the position of the hole indicated to him; if a player's ball strike the flagstick, which is held by or has been removed by himself, or his partner, or by either of their caddies, his side shall lose the hole; if the player's ball strike the flagstick which is held by or has been removed by an opponent or his caddie, the opponent's side shall lose the hole.

If a player or a caddie holds or removes the flagstick when a stroke is being played, such player or caddie shall be deemed to continue to hold the flagstick until the ball comes to rest.

If the ball rest against the flagstick which is in the hole, the player shall be entitled to remove the flagstick, and, if the ball fall into the hole, the player shall be deemed to have holed out at his last stroke.

In stroke competition when a ball lying within 20 yards of the hole is played, and strikes, or is stopped by the flagstick or the person standing at the hole, the penalty shall be two strokes. R. & A.

The penalty applies when the flagstick has been removed irrespective of whether it be actually held when struck. It also applies when the stick is attended irrespective of whether it is actually removed. U.S.G.A.

In match play there is no penalty for striking the flagstick when it has not been removed or is not attended by either side. U.S.G.A.

Displacing and Replacing of Balls

(2) If the player's ball knock the opponent's ball into the hole, the opponent shall be deemed to have holed out at his last stroke.

If the player's ball move the opponent's ball, the opponent, if he choose, may replace it, but this must be done before another stroke is played by either side.

If the player's ball stop on the spot formerly occupied by the opponent's ball, and the opponent declare his intention to replace his ball, the player shall first play another stroke, after which the opponent shall replace his ball.

See Stroke Rule 13 for penalty in stroke competitions. U.S.G.A.

Ball on Lip of Hole

(3) When the player has holed out and the opponent's ball has come to rest, the player may knock away the opponent's ball, conceding the half if holing at the odd, and claiming the hole if holing at the like.

If the player does not knock away the opponent's ball, and it fall into the hole, the opponent shall be deemed to have holed out at his last stroke.

If the opponent's ball has not been knocked away, the opponent shall play any subsequent stroke without delay.

RULE 33
Penalty of Loss of Hole Qualified by Half Previously Gained

When a player has holed out and his opponent has been left with a stroke for the half, nothing that the player who has holed out can do shall deprive him of the half which he has already gained, but if the player thereafter incur any penalty under the Rules of Golf he shall concede the half of the hole to his opponent.

GENERAL PENALTY

RULE 34

Loss of the Hole

Where no penalty for the breach of a rule or local rule is stated, the penalty shall be the loss of the hole.

Penalty in stroke play—Two strokes.

DISPUTES

RULE 35

Claims, when and how Made

If a dispute arise on any point, a claim must be made before the players strike off from the next teeing ground, or, in the case of the last hole of the round, before they leave the putting green. If the referee has been appointed or has been agreed upon by the players his decision shall be final; if no referee has been appointed the players have the right of determining to whom the point shall be referred, but should they not agree, either side may have an agreed statement referred officially through the secretary of the club, to the Rules of Golf Committee, whose decision shall be final. If the point in dispute be not covered by the Rules of Golf, the arbiters shall decide it by equity.

SPECIAL RULES FOR STROKE COMPETITIONS

STROKE RULE 1

The Winner

(1) In stroke competitions the competitor who holes the stipulated round or rounds in the fewest strokes shall be the winner.

The Rules of Golf Committee is of the opinion that it is hardly possible to play match and score play at the same time in a satisfactory manner, or without infringing rules. R. & A.

Order of Play

(2) Unless otherwise sanctioned in exceptional circumstances by the committee, competitors shall play in couples; if from any cause there be a single competitor, the committee shall either provide him with a player who shall mark for him, or select a marker for him and allow him to compete alone, or allow him to compete with another couple.

The order and times of starting should when possible, be determined by ballot.

STROKE RULE 2

Not to Discontinue Play

(1) Competitors shall start in the order and at the times arranged by the committee. They shall not discontinue play nor delay to start on account of bad weather or for any reason whatever, except such as the committee may consider satisfactory.

Penalty—Disqualification.

NOTE—If a competitor thinks he is endangered by lightning, he may discontinue play or delay to start, without penalty. If he does so without specific permission from the committee he should report it to the committee as soon as possible. Competitors are urged to seek proper shelter and committees are urged to do everything possible to help protect competitors in the event of lightning. U.S.G.A.

Course Unplayable

(2) If the committee consider that the course is not in a playable condition, or that insufficient light renders the proper playing of the game impossible, it shall at any time have power to declare play null and void.

STROKE RULE 3

Ties, how and when Decided

If the lowest scores be made by two or more competitors the tie or ties shall be decided as the committee may determine. The committee shall appoint the day and time for the decision of the ties.

STROKE RULE 4

New Holes

(1) New holes should be made on the day on which stroke competitions begin.

Practice on Day of Competition

(2) On the day or days of the competition no competitor shall practice before starting by playing on or on to, any of the putting greens, nor shall be intentionally play at any hole of the stipulated round which is within his reach.

Penalty—Disqualification.

For practice strokes and swings, see Notes to Rule 1.

STROKE RULE 5

The Scores, how Kept

(1) The score for each hole shall be kept by a marker or by each competitor acting as a marker noting the other's score. Should more than one marker keep a score each shall sign the part of the score for which he is responsible. The scores should be called out after each hole. On completion of the stipulated round the card shall be signed by the marker and the competitor shall see that it is handed in as soon as reasonably possible.

Penalty—Disqualification.

Scoring cards should be issued with the date and the player's name entered on the card.

A caddie cannot be considered a "marker." Under urgent and exceptional conditions, however, the committee may alter this interpretation. R. & A.

The penalty only applies to the competitor whose score was returned incorrectly and does not apply to the competitor who acted as a marker. U.S.G.A.

Marking and Addition of Scores

(2) No alteration can be made on any card after it has been returned. If it be found that a competitor has returned a score lower than that actually played, he shall be disqualified. For the additions of the scores marked the committee shall be responsible.

The penalty only applies to the competitor whose score was returned incorrectly and does not apply to the competitor who acted as marker. U.S.G.A.

NOTE — Each competitor is solely responsible for the correctness of the score reported for each hole. At the conclusion of his round a player must himself take his card, signed by the marker, check it, settle any doubtful question with the committee and then hand it in. It may not thereafter be altered. U.S.G.A.

Committee to Decide Doubtful Penalties

(3) If, on the completion of the stipulated round, a player is doubtful whether he has incurred a penalty at any hole, he may submit his scoring card with a report of the circumstances either verbal or in writing as the committee may decide. The committee shall then determine what penalty, if any, has been incurred.

DOUBT AS TO RIGHTS — In stroke play only, when a competitor is doubtful of his rights, he may: (1) Play out the hole with the ball from where it lies and, at the same time, complete the play of the hole with a second ball under what he believes to be his rights under the Rules for the given situation. (2) On completing the round he must report the facts immediately to the committee. If it be found that the Rules allow play in such manner as he played the second ball, his score with the second ball must be his score for the hole. To play a second ball in these circumstances constitutes an election to score with that ball if the Rules permit. If the Rules do not allow play as the second ball was played, then the score with the original ball is the score for the hole. (The sole purpose of this ruling is to enable a player to avoid risk of disqualification when doubtful of his rights; a player is not permitted to play in two ways and then choose his score.) (3) Before playing a stroke with either ball under this ruling, the player must announce to his marker (scorer) his intention to play both the original ball and a second ball. (NOTE — The above privilege of playing a second ball does not exist in match play.) U.S.G.A.

RULES FOR PLAY IN STROKE COMPETITIONS

STROKE RULE 6

Advice

A competitor shall not ask for nor take any action which may result in his receiving advice (Definition 2) except from his caddie.

NOTE. — A fellow-competitor is not a partner.

Penalty—Disqualification.

STROKE RULE 7

The Honour

(1) The honour shall be taken as in match play, but if a competitor by mistake play out of turn, no penalty shall be incurred, and the stroke cannot be recalled.

Playing Outside of Limits of Teeing Ground

(2) If at any hole a competitor play his first stroke from outside the limits of the teeing ground, he shall count that stroke, tee a ball, and play his second stroke from within these limits.

Penalty—Disqualification.

STROKE RULE 8

Must Hole out with Own Ball

(1) A competitor shall hole out with his own ball at every hole under penalty of disqualification.

See Definition 18 and note.
In order to avoid disqualification under this subdivision 1, a player must proceed under subdivision 2 of this Stroke Rule 8 before striking off from the next teeing ground. U.S.G.A.

Playing with Wrong Ball

(2) If a competitor play a stroke or strokes with a ball other than his own he shall incur a penalty of two strokes. He shall then play his own ball.

For practice strokes and swings, see Notes to Rule 1.

Exception in Hazards

(3) In a hazard, if a competitor play a stroke or strokes with a ball other than his own and the mistake be discovered before he has played a stroke with the wrong ball from outside the limits of the hazard, he shall incur no penalty provided he then play his own ball.

Penalty—Disqualification.
U.S.G.A. recommends that each competitor place an identification mark upon his ball.

STROKE RULE 9

Ball Striking or Moved by Another Player

If a competitor's ball strike or be stopped by another player, or his clubs, or his caddie, it is a rub of the green, except as provided for in Stroke Rule 13 (1), and the ball shall be played from where it lies. If a competitor's ball which is at rest be accidentally moved by another competitor, or his caddie, or his clubs, or his ball, or any outside agency except wind, a ball shall be placed as near as possible to the spot where it lay.

Penalty—Disqualification.

Ball Striking the Player, etc.

If a player's ball strike himself, or his caddie or his clubs, he shall incur a penalty of two strokes.

STROKE RULE 10

Allowed to Lift Another Player's Ball

A competitor may have any other player's ball played or lifted, at the option of its owner, if he find that it interferes with his play.

STROKE RULE 11

Lifting Ball

A ball may be lifted from any place on the course. If a player lift a ball under the provisions of this Rule he shall either

(1) play a ball as provided for in Rule 22 or

(2) tee and play a ball under penalty of two strokes behind the place from which the ball was lifted; if this be impossible he shall tee and play a ball under penalty of two strokes as near as possible to the place from which the ball was lifted but not nearer to the hole.

In preparing a tee as above authorised, the player is exempted from the restrictions imposed by Rule 15.

Penalty—Disqualification.

STROKE RULE 12

Lifting for Identification

For the purpose of identification, a competitor may at any time lift and replace his ball on the spot from which it was lifted in the presence of the player with whom he is competing.

Ball Unfit for Play

If a ball be so damaged as to be unfit for play, the player may change it on intimating to his fellow-competitor or marker his intention to do so. Mud adhering to a ball shall not be considered as making it unfit for play.

Penalty—Two strokes.
See Definition 18 and note.
Whether or not a ball be unfit for play is a question of fact, and must be decided by the referee. If there be no referee, the question if arising in stroke play must be decided as provided in Stroke Rules 5 (3) and 16.

STROKE RULE 13

Play Within 20 Yards of Hole
Ball Striking Flagstick, etc.

(1) When a competitor's ball lying within twenty yards of the hole is played and strikes, or is stopped by, the flagstick or the person standing at the hole, the penalty shall be two strokes.

Neglect on the part of the person standing at the hole does not exempt the competitor from incurring the penalty. R. & A.

Ball Striking Fellow-Competitor's Ball

(2) When both balls are on the putting green, if a competitor's ball strike the ball of the player with whom he is competing, the competitor shall incur a penalty of two strokes, and the ball which was struck shall be at once replaced. (See Stroke Rule 10.)

Nearer Ball May be Lifted

(3) The competitor whose ball is the farther from the hole may have the ball which is nearer to the hole lifted or played at the option of its owner. If the latter refuse to comply with this Rule when requested to do so, he shall be disqualified.

Ball Nearer Hole of Assistance to Player

(4) If the competitor whose ball is the nearer to the hole consider that his ball might be of assistance to the player with whom he is competing, he should lift it or play first.

Ball Lifted when Player's Ball in Motion

(5) If the competitor whose ball is the nearer to the hole lift his ball while the player's ball is in motion, he shall incur a penalty of two strokes.

Ball Lifted before Holed Out

(6) If a competitor or his caddie pick up his ball from the putting green before it is holed out (except as provided for above), he shall, before he has struck off from the next teeing ground, or, in the case of the last hole of the round, before he has left the putting green, be permitted to replace the ball under penalty of two strokes.

STROKE RULE 14

General Penalty

Where in the Rules of Golf the penalty for the breach of any rule is the loss of the hole, in stroke competitions the penalty shall be the loss of two strokes, except where otherwise provided for in these Special Rules.

STROKE RULE 15

General Rule

The Rules of Golf, so far as they are not at variance with these Special Rules, shall apply to stroke competitions.

STROKE RULE 16

Disputes, how Decided

If a dispute arise on any point it shall be decided by the committee, whose decision shall be final, unless an appeal be made to the Rules of Golf Committee, as provided for in Rule 35.

RULES FOR STROKE PLAY FOURSOME COMPETITIONS

The Special Rules for Stroke Competitions shall apply to stroke play foursome competitions, and where the context so admits the word "competitor" shall be held to include the "partner."

RULES FOR PAR AND BOGEY COMPETITIONS

A bogey competition is a form of stroke competition in which play is against a fixed score at each hole of the stipulated round or rounds.

The reckoning is made as in match play and the winner is the competitor who is most successful in the aggregate of holes. The Rules for Stroke Competitions shall apply with the following exceptions: —

(1) Any hole for which a competitor makes no return shall be regarded as a loss. The marker shall only be responsible for the marking of the correct number of strokes at each hole at which a competitor makes a score either equal to or less than the fixed score, under handicap.

(2) Any breach of rule which entails the penalty of disqualification, shall only disqualify the competitor for the hole at which the breach of rule occurred; but a competitor shall not be exempted from general disqualification imposed by Stroke Rules 2 (1), 4 (2), and 5 (1) and (2) provided that Stroke Rule 5 (2) shall not operate when a mistake in the marking of a card does not affect the result of the hole.

NOTE. — The holes at which strokes are to be given or taken should be indicated on the scoring card.

The United States Golf Association recommends that each competitor be allowed seven-eights of his full handicap.

RULES FOR THREE-BALL, BEST BALL AND FOUR-BALL MATCHES
GENERAL

(1) Any player may have any ball in the match lifted or played, at the option of its owner, if he consider that it might interfere with or be of assistance to a player or side, but this is only permissible before the player has played his stroke.

(2) If a player's ball move any other ball in the match, the moved ball must be replaced as near as possible to the spot where it lay, without penalty.

(3) Through the green a player shall incur no penalty for playing when an opponent should have done so, and the stroke shall not be recalled.

On the putting green the stroke may be recalled by an opponent, but no penalty shall be incurred.

THREE-BALL MATCHES

(4) During a three-ball match if no player is entitled at a teeing ground to claim the honour from both opponents, the same order of striking shall be followed as at the last teeing ground.

(5) In a three-ball match, if a player's ball strike or be moved by an opponent or an opponent's caddie or clubs, that opponent shall lose the hole to the player. As regards the other opponent the occurrence shall be treated as a rub of the green.

BEST BALL AND FOUR-BALL MATCHES

(6) Balls belonging to the same side shall be played in the order the side deems best.

(7) If a player's ball strike, or be moved by an opponent or an opponent's caddie or clubs, the opponent's side shall lose the hole.

In stroke competition it is a rub of the green, and the ball shall be played from where it lies except as provided for in Stroke Rule 13 (2). See Stroke Rule 9. U.S.G.A.

(8) If a player's ball (the player being one of a side) strike, or be stopped by himself or his partner, or either of their caddies or clubs, only that player shall be disqualified for that hole.

(9) If a player play a stroke with his partner's ball, and the mistake be discovered and intimated to the other side before an opponent has played another stroke, the player shall be disqualified for that hole, and his partner shall drop a ball as near as possible to the spot from which his ball was played, without penalty. If the mistake be not discovered till after the opponent has played a stroke, the player's side shall lose the hole.

(10) In all other cases where a player would by the Rules of Golf incur the loss of the hole, he shall be disqualified for that hole, but the disqualification shall not apply to his partner.

NOTE—If a player play a stroke with a ball of anyone not engaged in the match Rule 20 (2) governs, except that if the mistake be not discovered and so intimated until after an opponent has played his next stroke the player's side shall lose the hole. U.S.G.A.

FORM AND MAKE OF GOLF CLUBS AND BALLS
CLUBS

The United States Golf Association will not sanction any substantial departure from the traditional and accepted form and make of golf clubs which, in its opinion, consist of a plain shaft and a head which do not contain any mechanical contrivance, such as springs; it also regards as illegal the use of such clubs as those of the mallet-headed type, or such clubs as have the neck, or shaft, so bent as to produce a similar effect.

Club faces shall not embody any degree of concavity or more than one angle of loft, and shall not bear any lines, dots, or other markings with sharp or rough edges made for the obvious purpose of putting a cut on the ball.

Markings on iron clubs shall conform with U.S.G.A. specifications.

(Specifications have been issued to manufacturers. Players in doubt as to the legality of their iron clubs are advised to consult the U.S.G.A. or manufacturers.)

Insets in the faces of iron clubs are not allowed.

The following general considerations will guide the Rules of Golf Committee in interpreting the above: —

1. The head of a golf club shall be so constructed that the length of the head from the back of the heel to the toe shall be greater than the breadth from the face to the back of the head.

2. The shaft shall be fixed to the heel or to a neck, socket or hose in line with the heel or to a point opposite the heel, either to right or left, when the club is soled in the ordinary position for play.

3. The shaft of a putter may be fixed at any point in the head between the heel and a line terminating at the center of the sole.

BALLS

The weight of the ball shall be not greater than 1.620 ounces avoirdupois, and the size not less than 1.680 inches in diameter. The velocity of the ball shall be not greater than 250 feet per second when measured on the U.S.G.A.'s apparatus; the temperature of the ball when so tested shall be 75 degrees Fahrenheit; a maximum tolerance of 2% will be allowed on any ball in such velocity test.

————

RECOMMENDATIONS FOR LOCAL RULES

When necessary local rules should be made for such obstructions as rushes, bushes, trees, hedges, fences, gates, railways, walls, pumps, boundary stones, notice boards, and drains, for such difficulties as rabbit scrapes, hoof marks and other damage caused to the course by animals, for such local conditions as the existence of mud which may be held to interfere with the proper playing of the game and for the preservation of the course.

Ball, when "Dropped"; when "Placed"

When a ball is lifted under a local rule, the Rules of Golf Committee recommends that if it is to be played from "through the green," it should be dropped; if it is to be played in the putting green of the hole that is being played, it should be placed. The provisions of Rule 8 should be applied.

NOTE. — For a ball out of bounds see Rule 23.

INDEX FOR RULES

INDEX FOR RULES

INDEX FOR RULES

INDEX FOR RULES

INDEX FOR RULES

INDEX FOR RULES

RULES GOVERNING ELIGIBILITY
TO AMATEUR CLASSIFICATIONS

The following Regulations shall govern the eligibility of players to compete as amateurs in competitions held under the auspices of the United States Golf Association.

The Executive Committee of the United States Golf Association expressly reserves the right to refuse the entry into any competition under its jurisdiction of any player, amateur or professional, who in its opinion has acted in a manner detrimental to the best interests or the spirit of the game.

Section 1. Acts After Eighteenth Birthday.
The following Regulations—Section 1 (a to i) — apply only to the acts of a player committed subsequent to his eighteenth birthday or, in the case of a player who has been reinstated to Amateur Classification (see Section 4), subsequent to the date of such reinstatement.

A player shall be deemed to be ineligible to compete as an amateur:

(a) If he has received compensation for acting in the capacity of a caddie; for employment as an assistant to a professional; as an employee in a golf shop engaged in making, repairing or cleaning golf clubs; as a green-keeper charged with the maintenance of a golf course or his assistant (bona fide manual workers excepted); as a caddie-master or his assistant.

(b) If he has received compensation for giving instructions in playing the game. These Regulations include oral and written instruction, instruction by demonstration and by pictures, and are applicable whether such instruction has been given to groups or to individuals. Exempt from this provision are full-time members of the faculties of recognized institutions of learning, only a minor part of whose duties include instruction in golf. To enjoy this exemption, however, the teacher must confine his instruction to regularly enrolled students of the institution by which he is employed.

(c) If he has played in a match, a tournament or an exhibition with the intention or hope of accepting money or its equivalent as a prize or as compensation.

(d) If, because of his skill as a golfer, he has received a salary or remuneration directly or indirectly from any firm dealing in goods relating to the playing of the game.

(e) If he has accepted without payment golf balls, clubs or golf merchandise from a manufacturer or a dealer in golf equipment or their agents.

(f) If he has received or contracted to receive compensation for lending his name or his likeness for the advertisement or the sale of anything except as he may be a dealer, a manufacturer, or an inventor thereof.

(g) If he has received or contracted to receive compensation for permitting his name to be advertised or published as the author of books or articles on golf of which he is not actually the author.

(h) If, because of his skill as a golfer, he has accepted membership or privileges in a club under conditions not ordinarily available to other members unless such membership and/or privileges have been awarded as purely and deservedly honorary and in recognition of an outstanding national performance or contribution to golf.

(i) If he has accepted money covering his expenses in connection with golf competitions or golf exhibitions except from one on whom he normally depends for support; provided that he may accept a reasonable amount of expense money in the following four specific instances:

(1) As a member of the Walker Cup Team, but such expense money may be accepted from only the U.S.G.A.

(2) As a member of the Curtis Cup Team, but such expense money may be accepted from only the U.S.G.A.

(3) As a qualified contestant in the U.S.G.A. Amateur Public Links Championship.

(4) As a member of a team regularly organized as a part of the athletic activities of a recognized institution of learning and competing under the auspices of an association existing for the purpose of conducting such competitions.

Section 2. Acts Before Eighteenth Birthday.
The following Regulations — Section 2 (a to c) — apply only to the acts of a player committed previous to his eighteenth birthday.

(a) A player shall be deemed to be ineligible to compete as an amateur during the period in which he is engaged in any of those activities appearing herein in Section 1 (a to i).

(b) A player, irrespective of his previous activities, shall be deemed automatically to have become eligible to compete in amateur competitions upon attaining his eighteenth birthday, subject, however, to the provisions of Section 2 (c) immediately following:

(c) If anyone whose golfing activities have conflicted with these Regulations shall cease such activities prior to his eighteenth birthday and so declare himself, he shall automatically become eligible to Amateur Classification; provided, however, that one who thus ceases such activities and so declares himself and who, thereby, subsequently competes as an amateur shall be deemed to have been reinstated. (Note: A player may not be reinstated more than once. See Section 4 (d).)

Section 3. Prizes for Amateurs.
It is the opinion of the United States Golf Association that the best interests of the game of golf will be served if prizes for amateur competitions be limited to objects of greater symbolic and less intrinsic value. It advised particularly against the offering of prizes of the following character:

(a) Those of unusual money value (a top limit in value of one hundred dollars is suggested).

(b) Those whose nature makes them readily convertible into cash.

(c) Orders on mercantile establishments which fail to limit the purpose to which the orders may be put.

Section 4. Reinstatement to Amateur Classification.
(a) Each application for reinstatement to Amateur Classification shall be considered on its own merits and the Executive Committee of the United States Golf Association expressly reserves the right to disapprove any such application for reasons which it deems to be sufficient.

(b) An applicant for reinstatement to Amateur Classification shall prepare his application, in duplicate, on forms designed for that purpose by the United States Golf Association, which will furnish such forms upon request. The application shall be submitted, in duplicate, to an officer of a responsible sectional golf association in whose district the applicant resides. The said officer of the sectional association shall endorse upon the form, in the space provided, the recommendations of his association and shall forward both copies to the office of the United States Golf Association. The United States Golf Association shall take action upon the application, it shall appropriately endorse both copies and it shall forward the duplicate copy to the applicant, as provided in Section 4 (g) herein. The duplicate copy shall be the applicant's notification of the action of the United States Golf Association.

(c) Each application for reinstatement to Amateur Classification shall be accompanied by a letter from each of four responsible persons who shall vouch for the reputation of the applicant and, within his judgment, the accuracy of the applicant's statements. These four letters shall accompany the application to the sectional association whose endorsement is sought and thence to the office of the United States Golf Association.

(d) A player may not be reinstated to Amateur Classification more than once.

(e) An applicant shall not become eligible for reinstatement to Amateur Classification until a probationary period of two consecutive years shall have elapsed during which period he shall have at all times conducted himself in such a manner as to qualify for such Classification under these Regulations.

(f) A player shall be ineligible for reinstatement to Amateur Classification if through any five-year period subsequent to his eighteenth birthday he has engaged in activities of a character to exclude him from Amateur Classification under these Regulations.

(g) Thirty days shall elapse between the date on which a completed application shall be received at the office of the United States Golf Association and the date on which the Amateur Classification of the applicant may be restored. However, an application may be tendered to the United States Golf Association prior to the expiration of the applicant's probationary period. Such an application shall be deemed to have been received either as of the date on which it shall actually have been received or as of the date thirty days prior to the expiration of the applicant's probationary period, whichever of the two is the later.

Section 5. Amateur Golfers in Exhibition Matches. An amateur golfer may take part in an exhibition match for which admission is charged provided that the exhibition has been arranged primarily for the benefit of and the net proceeds actually are to be paid to a recognized charitable institution. Professionals appearing in such matches may be paid appropriate amounts for their services, and the sponsor may be reimbursed only to the extent of its actual expenses. The expenses of the sponsor must be certified by one empowered by the sponsor to issue such certification.

Section 6. Professionals as Club Members. Any club may include in its membership a professional golfer or one who for any reason is ineligible to play in amateur competitions, and the Amateur Classification of its other members shall not thereby be affected.

PROTECTION OF PERSONS AGAINST LIGHTNING

As there have been many deaths and injuries from lightning on golf courses, the United States Golf Association urges all golfers, sponsors of golf and caddies to take every precaution for the protection of persons against lightning.

Discontinuing and Resuming Play

The U.S.G.A. has adopted the following procedure and recommends that every local Committee do likewise; the U.S.G.A. especially suggests that players be made aware that they have advance right to stop play if they feel that lightning threatens them:

In stroke play: The following footnote has been added to Stroke Rule 2 (1), effective 1942: "NOTE – If a competitor thinks he is endangered by lightning, he may discontinue play or delay to start, without penalty. If he does so without specific permission from the committee, he should report it to the committee as soon as possible. Competitors are urged to seek proper shelter and committees are urged to do everything possible to help protect competitors in the event of lightning. U.S.G.A."

In match play: Players taking shelter by agreement cannot be disqualified under any specific rule governing match play, unless, of course, they unfairly delay a competition.

The Committee will give the following signals to indicate certain of the times when play may be discontinued and resumed (but, as stated above, players may discontinue if they consider themselves endangered by lightning even though the signal may not have been given):

Discontinue play – Three consecutive notes of siren, repeated.

Resume play – One prolonged note of siren, repeated.

As to discontinuing play, a player may either:

(a) Complete the play of the hole on which he is engaged; or

(b) Lift his ball, without penalty; if the ball does not lie in a hazard, the player may place a peg tee or a similar marker firmly in the ground as near as possible to where the ball lay, or, if the ball lie in a hazard, he should note carefully its lie and position so as to replace the ball therein upon resuming play.

Suggestions for Sheltering

The following suggestions are made in the National Bureau of Standards Handbook No. 21, 1937, p. 2:

(a) Do not go out of doors or remain out during thunderstorms unless it is necessary. Stay inside of a building where it is dry, preferably away from fireplaces, stoves and other metal objects.

(b) If there is any choice of shelter, choose in the following order:
1. Large metal or metal-frame buildings.
2. Dwellings or other buildings which are protected against lightning.
3. Large unprotected buildings.
4. Small unprotected buildings.

(c) If remaining out of doors is unavoidable,
1. Keep away from
   (1) Small sheds and shelters if in an exposed location.
   (2) Isolated trees.
   (3) Wire fences.
   (4) Hilltops and wide open spaces.

2. Seek shelter in
   (1) A cave.
   (2) A depression in the ground.
   (3) A deep valley or canyon.
   (4) The foot of a steep or overhanging cliff.
   (5) Dense woods.
   (6) A grove of trees.

NOTE BY UNITED STATES GOLF ASSOCIATION — It is understood that the elevation of golf clubs or umbrellas above one's normal height is dangerous.

It is suggested that an ample supply of notices similar to this be posted at courses. Copies of this notice in poster form may be obtained from the U.S.G.A.

DIRECTIONS
FOR COMPUTING PAR

MEN'S PAR

Par 3................up to 250 yards, inclusive
Par 4................251 to 445 yards, inclusive
Par 5................446 to 600 yards, inclusive
Par 6................601 yards and over

Par means perfect play without flukes and under ordinary weather conditions, always allowing two strokes on each putting green.

The above figures are not arbitrary, because some allowance should be made for the configuration of the ground and any other difficult or unusual conditions. So also should be considered the severity of the hazards, especially on a hole where the par is doubtful.

Each hole should be measured horizontally from the middle of the tee to the center of the green, following the planned line of play.

WOMEN'S PAR

Par 3................up to 210 yards, inclusive
Par 4................211 to 400 yards, inclusive
Par 5................401 to 575 yards, inclusive
Par 6................576 yards and over